TOI

We are all children of the universe. No one is better or more
important than another. We are all important and perfect.
And yet in the scheme of things all we really need to do is
walk our path and do the best we can. Why are humans so
judgmental? This does not happen on the other side or in
other realms (usually). This judgment and individuality
happens mostly here on planet earth. This is a dense way of
thinking and being but it is where we are right now and all
we can do is walk our path despite the inclines, the rocky
twists and turns, and the mud. We are here now and
working in this realm (that we are aware of) and while here
we do our best and shine our brightest. This is not judge-
worthy; this is living the good life and one we can be proud
of. This is not to say that if you feel you haven't "done
enough" that you've failed. Let that concept go. Just start
from today; start from this breath. Keep breathing and
loving and growing and try to smile through it all. There is
denseness here but with the changes throughout our
time/space, we are morphing into something more;
something better. Today we are here and we must connect
to the earth and to the sun and stars for a good balance of
body/mind/spirit. Do your best and stay as connected as
possible. Take one step at a time and keep trying; keep
smiling; stay faithful and feel blessed. We are who we've
been waiting for; wait no more: BE THAT.

LoveNLight to you on this very fine day.

TODAY'S MESSAGE

Life is full of complications and contradictions. We are living in duality (if we want to). There are also great miracles and beauty here on earth: what are you going to focus upon? When we view life in the terms of duality we often feel like things are out of balance and that one side is "winning," and another losing. If we live in the miracles and beauty of life, then we care not about the duality, for we find beauty in it ALL. Let us find beauty and miracles in ALL THAT IS. It is up to our mind/thoughts and our perception and our open heart to decide how we are going to live this thing we called life. Duality? Or Beauty In All Things? You must choose and follow-through. Be in the flow of the beauty/miracles and more will become present. Let go of the judgment (the duality) for it is not up to an individual soul to judge, for each of us have limited knowledge on all topics. We do not have universal knowledge on anything. Though, we can tap into unlimited knowledge, if we would like, by finding the super-conscious-all-that-is, and going there. The beauty there is that as you are tapped in, the judgment ceases and we just bathe in the light. Let us find the light/super-conscious/all-that-is as often as possible. It is up to each of us to choose to go there. No media or friend will take you there. Only you ~ as you go within. That is where the fruit is. Within ~ go there ~ and all will become available.

LOVENLIGHT!

TODAY'S MESSAGE

Get excited! Why not? You might as well enjoy living in this realm called earth-life and while you are at it you might as well get excited for the prospects as well. Many dreams can come true here. Many nightmares as well, so do consider where you focus. If you are always focused on the negative then more of that will come into your experience: the universe won't let you down and will give you just what you see/perceive/dream. So let us just say for a moment that we shall live this life to the fullest and with great excitement and anticipation as well as appreciation for the process. It is all a process and many lessons can be learned here. Maybe one of our lessons is finding the joy of living; regardless of the circumstances. Like the dolphins ~ who are so joyous and happy in their day to day experiences ~ we can "jump" for joy and reach for the stars. We can keep jumping and being joyous regardless of where we find ourselves after making such an attempt. Stay in the love-zone is the idea here. Let the old fade away; wash away so that you can be born anew in the spirit of celebration. There is much to celebrate here. Regardless of how dense it may seem at times or how real life does affect us all (sickness, death, loss, fear, etc.) let us keep jumping for joy so that the dolphins and the universe and the higher powers will laugh and jump and celebrate with us. To love and light and have a super perfect day (regardless).

God Bless.

TODAY'S MESSAGE

Today is like every day, though today, and right now, is all you have so make it extraordinary! Right now your day may not seem so special or wonderful but that can be turned around with a change of perspective. Your day can be more special/important the more you are "in it." So again, the BE-ing, as has been mentioned before. Also, BE-ing from your heart-space is a great place to work and play from as well. Feeling and sensing and encompassing all that is as you go about your day will make it super crazy wonderful and/or important, anyway. This is the idea that the more we work through awareness, the more we are BE-ing and living consciously. The more we live in higher consciousness awareness, the less karma we accumulate along the way for now we are breaking patterns and acting (not reacting). Living in this way also helps us identify the patterns and let them go. Living more consciously allows us to live more authentically as well for as we are more and more conscious, the less games we play with ourselves and others and the more present and real we are for ourselves and those around us. This is wonderful and is simply a practice. Just because you are BE-ing today, doesn't mean you'll remember to BE tomorrow. Life is like that: it allows us much practice. Isn't that wonderful? As like any practice, however, it becomes more natural as we practice. And what could be more natural then to BE YOU? Yes, just be that wonderful you and stay open in mind/heart/body/spirit. Life is for the practice and the joy. Do find some of both today.

And God Bless, now and all-ways.

TODAY'S MESSAGE

Everything in its own timing. We cannot rush the universe and sometimes what we think we need, we do not need. And what we think we want, we are still unsure, or not yet clear. There are many things we can gain while here on planet earth. Just because you think you need a certain thing to happen at a certain time ~ that may not be beneficial to you and your life's path. There may not be clarity just yet around those ideas, see? This is where faith comes in, which has been said before. This is where hope comes in as well as a long-standing agreement that one works WITH the All That Is, the higher calling, the universe; not against it. We need not push and pull and we need not fret. Be open and clear about your desires and then allow. One must allow an opening in one's life to accommodate and integrate the new. Now just may not be the perfect time for your manifestation to come to fruition. Life is funny like that. The main point here is to not give up hope and to not give up on your creation vision. There is enough abundance and truth and light here on planet earth to fill your dreams. Be clear and be open and keep the faith. Stay strong in your hope-light. Stay vigilant in your practice of The Way. Many are struggling and are blinded by why. Be grateful for your connection and your vision and oneness with source. All is perfect, as are you.

Chins up and stay strong!

Blessed Be.

TODAY'S MESSAGE

There are so many ideas we can explore here on planet earth (and elsewhere). We are here to learn and grow. It is nice to find an "ideal" to work with throughout our day/week/year. Edgar Cayce often spoke of creating an ideal and working from there. This ideal can be one of love, integrity, balance, fairness, openness, etc. One's topics for lessons can be as varied as the individual. The idea of the ideal and the topics for lessons, here, is that we can "work on ourselves" as we go about our day. We can BE what we wish to see in the world, as they like to say. Be peace, be generous, be a savior. We can do whatever we want and if we want to advance in our spirituality, having an ideal or a topic for learning lessons is a great way to go about it. If we are here to learn and grow AND we create our ideals and topics for learning, then we go about our day more consciously. Going about life more consciously allows us to break through those triggers we once reacted to unconsciously. Now if we react in the old way, then at least we will notice this, as we are living more consciously. Then our "issues" or "triggers" can be recognized, evaluated and resolved. Why do we typically act in a certain way when we would really like to act in another way? These things can be worked on through self-evaluation as we live and play with the outside world. Who do you want to be? Create an ideal and work and play toward this ideal person. You are on your way and life is perfect. Allow your world to be your playground and your teacher and enjoy the restructuring of self toward the ideal of your being.

God Bless. LOVENLIGHT!

TODAY'S MESSAGE

Stand your ground when it comes to your faith, but go with the flow, as well. Sounds contradictory but these two things can happen in tandem. Allowing your body/mind/spirit to FLOW with the universe is so beneficial. Staying strong in your faith and power and growth/knowledge; staying on YOUR PATH is also very important right now as the world, at large, can seem a bit topsy-turvy at times and "others" (friends/family/the outside world) can be acting extremely, as well. So REGARDLESS of what is happening you can stay on your path of light and love. Find your heart ~ that helps lead you back to your path. Allow the fear of the outside world to stay clear of your energy/love/system. Allow the All That Is to guide you through the universal properties of synchronicity and flow. Ask and be directed. Ask and receive. Be open to the answers and direction and move forward on your path. Now is a time of vigilance when it comes to practicing what we've been taught in the way of spiritual truths: walking the talk, so to speak. But regardless, it is all good and all is well in the process of enlightenment. That is where we are going, you know. It is time to lighten up! And all is perfect. Worry not about the others on THEIR path; focus on yours and stay strong. Of course assist others when available and directed to do so, but again, self-healing/focus/growth is paramount during these times of change.

God Bless.

TODAY'S MESSAGE

We are each alone; and yet we are not alone. It is more of a
perception than anything else. It is more of a sense of
freedom we like to create for ourselves. Of course "our
path" is each individualized and even then we cross paths
and there is a "support" there from our brothers and sisters
and even our friends and "enemies." The idea here is that
even though we feel "singular" on our path and in our life,
there is so much support that we often don't see and/or feel.
There is support from the higher realms. There is support
from our "higher self." There is support from the earth
below our feet and from the sun above. The plants and
animals support us ~ have you ever thought of that? The
wind supports us; the fire; the sun and the moon. So much
support and yet we feel so all alone at times! Why is that?
Do know you are not alone. Do know you are truly loved.
Even if you think of "just" your "higher self" or your soul
loves you; even if you can imagine a guardian angel loving
and caring for you ~ that may just be the turn-around to get
you out of the place of singular –thinking; especially if that
mindset is taking a downward spiral (as they often do). Let
us, today, feel love from something greater than ourselves.

Let us realize that many are routing for us.

TODAY'S MESSAGE

Be where you are: where ever that may be. It may not always be the most pleasant setting, where you are right now, but the more you are "in" it, the more you can find gratitude for all that is. Every day won't be perfect and every second isn't either, of course, but the more you are "there" the better things can flow. It is truly all about gratitude: gratitude and appreciation of ALL THINGS. Allowing with freedom, grace, and ease (as has been said before) is lovely AND the idea of "allowing" all that is LOVINGLY, and WILLING in your presence is perfect. This idea is strong if one can truly "get into it." Look at the animals and the natural world. They are living NOW and they are allowing and they are being and all is perfect. For much of the natural world, needs are based on "the now" and when we are in the now, much of what we think we need seems to vanish. This is because much of what we think we need is simply conditioned/programmed in us from society and/or our surroundings and our up-bringing. To release the past and live in the now and allow all that is to be lovingly and willing endured/enjoyed is heaven. Let's go there now. And now. And now. Stay in the flow and enjoy! (in joy).

God Bless and

Thank You for practicing these concepts.

TODAY'S MESSAGE

Love is the fabric that binds us all. We all feel we are alone
here on planet earth; that it is self against the world, but that
is not the case at all. Love weaves its magic and we are one.
All-That-Is, is woven together by love, to make the great
fabric called life. If you want to tap into All That Is, just find
the love-thread and go there. When you are living within the
fabric of love you will find your heart is the same as the
others: your family, your friends and your so called enemies.
The loving thread weaves us to those across the sea and
those in our back yard. It weaves life everlasting, as well.
We do not ever "lose" those who pass before us for our
thread of love binds us, see? Energy touches the soul as it is
energy, our bodies are energy, our minds and thoughts are
energy, etc. etc. We are all one; regardless of whether you
"feel it" or not. As you open your heart to the loving energy
of oneness, then you heal yourself and others. You don't
have to create this in another; your loving heart is all it takes.
You don't need to "sway" a person or make them see your
side: just open your heart and an understanding can be had.
We are together on this path called life as love weaves our
paths together. You are not alone. Sometimes you may
think you are but you are not. That is all one needs to know
to keep loving and trying. Thank you for your good (light)
work and God Bless.

LOVENLIGHT!

TODAY'S MESSAGE

Just Be. That is our job here on earth: to experience and BE in all that is. How beautiful is that? What would you like to be today? HOW would you like to be (live) in this experience right now? These are beautiful concepts and living in the present allows this to happen. Grounding down, into mother earth, helps in this regard, as well. Living a soul purpose is good and living to help others is lovely, but BE-ing is the main thing. How BIG do you want to be today? How HUMBLE? How BRAVE? There are many ideals you can work from today and picking an ideal and living it consciously can be so helpful in SEEING. What will you see, you may ask? Well, you may see certain old patterning that crops up for you. You may see misconceptions about self and others that you hold onto. One need not hold onto anything when they are in the BE-ing state, so just let that shit go. Release the fears, the anxiety and the negative self-talk. Release the idea that you need, or are required to act, in a certain way due to upbringing or societal norms. Let the old structures go and be in the infinite joyous oneness here on earth. Tap into the higher realms and give thanks for the opportunity. As you do, your heart will grow and the light from your heart and the others who are doing their self-work and who are just BE-ing in the love and light of God/Goddess/Oneness/Universe, will rise up and sweep the nations, the communities and the world at large. Your heart is so important for that to happen. And to think, all you need to do is to simply BE. LOVENLIGHT! And have a most blessed day.

TODAY'S MESSAGE

We are one: you and I and all that is. We could stop here if this idea can be fully recognized. But with existence the way it stands right here and now on planet earth we can see this has not been realized. "In the end," we will all realize this. Together we stand; divided we fall: this idea is vital. In the world right now there are many divisions. As groups we see each other as different; as separate. But this is not the case at all! We are one human family; one group soul: all trying to make it on our own. We can work in this way though as we do we are continuously put in situations to try to understand thy brothers and sister. There are wars and famine and heart-ache aplenty. In these times of pain and hardship, the idea of empathy and compassion reign. Let it reign. We need to identify with the oneness of humanity so that all can live a glorious life. Now there is division but it is just an illusion. Whether you believe in the oneness idea or not, it is our underlying existence, nonetheless. We are simply being put into these situations to finally understand. We ARE our brother's keeper. We ARE here to help others less fortunate. The race is not one against the rest of the world. The race is to bring all mankind together to finally "see" each other for who we really are: divine sparks of the divine creator. When we start to see, then the division becomes less and less for it is then we recognize the same spark in ourselves. Love is the ONLY answer. Try some love today and notice in others that beautiful spark that we often keep hidden. It is in the plants and trees and animals. It is in the oceans and skies. The sun shines divinely and we are one. God bless and have a great day.

TODAY'S MESSAGE

Don't race against time; transcend time and BE in this perfect moment. This is easier said than done for here on earth everything is measured in time: seconds, minutes, hours and days; a lifetime. Though what if we were infinite beings and this earth-life is simply one day or hour out of your infinite experience? That is an interesting concept. Nothing you have to "believe" in but a concept you can incorporate during your day to day. Instead of worrying about how much you can do in a day and how many things you can do in this minute ~ the idea that there is "all the time in the world" is a good place to be. This isn't to say to be lazy or whatnot; this is to say that your experience is truly right here and right now so do stop the worry of "I'm not doing enough" or "I shall run out of time." This RIGHT HERE and RIGHT NOW is the only time that matters. One can have many realizations and "enlightened ideas" in a fraction of a second so there is enough time for all that you are and all you wish to be. BEING in "the now" is the idea and letting the worry go of "that which was" or the feeling of "that which will never be" makes a more flowing life. For NOW is where the BEING lies so the rest doesn't really matter, see? Doing what you love and feeling joy in all you do is the key. This isn't egocentric for if you are happy, then your "existence" is happy. As your existence is happy then your "world-view" or view of life/living is happy and then all is perfect in the world, see? Be grateful and loving and have a blessed "now."

LOVENLIGHT!

TODAY'S MESSAGE

Be where you are when you are there. Be. Be The I AM
Presence of Everything for you are indeed that. The idea
here is to know this and live in that moment of the I AM; to
"claim it" so to speak. This may seem like it will slow you
down a bit and if that is the case then it is perfect. We, in
the western society, often run hither and yon and work work
work and even multi-task so we can do several items of work
at the same time. Unless you can bi-locate then you are not
in the I AM and in the PRESENT for the mind is many
other places. The idea here is to bring your focus on the one
place you are existing here, right now. The old adage of not
living in the past and not fretting over the future is the idea
here but also see too that we can be even MORE in the
present with the trinity: mind/body/spirit and that
alignment brings us to the divine presence and allows for the
current experiences to not only be enjoyed, but fully
absorbed and integrated into the body system. Again the
idea of having all your faculties (mind/body/spirit) present
for all things (not just body doing something and mind
elsewhere, see?). This is a great way to live and the only way
to truly BE. Allow the thoughts to come and allow the body
to move and allow your spirit to be connected to all that is.
You are divine. You know this but we are here to remind
you once again. YOU are part and parcel of the perfect I
AM Presence of Everything. So let's BE that today.

**God Bless Always; now and forever ~ in all your
glorious moments here on planet earth.**

TODAY'S MESSAGE

Our life experience can be grand indeed. Or, our life can be quiet and subtle. Much of our life experience can be altered by us through our sense of intention and free will. "What do I want to do with my life?" And "how do I see myself here in this experience?" Some of our lives seem to be more predestined, but it is said that we can often over ride anything in this experience, if we so want to, due to our free will. That being said, what can we do with this information? Thoughts today seem to indicate that we can be whatever we want to be and experience all that we can imagine. The visualizations, within you, have a huge effect on this process. If you continue to visualize yourself in lacking situations, then more lack will come your way. This idea of the law of attraction, as been said before, and it applies here as well. If we ask to have our karma cleared up with freedom grace and ease then that helps assist the process too. Though for that to occur we need to be open so we can see and feel and really "get" those lessons. Then those old programs, that you've come in with, will be less visualized and felt/kept in your body. Then more, new, exciting and dynamic visualizations can take their place. Those of where you want to be, not where you "have to be;" see? Clearing up the old in gentle steps and allowing new space for the grandeur to insist. Let that be our intention for today.

LOVEANDLIGHT

and

have a blessed day.

TODAY'S MESSAGE

Don't let other people's fear weigh you down. You are not responsible for other people's happiness. Yes, we can each do our part to help relieve the weight of the world on other's psyche, but it is ultimately up to each individual to think and act in their own way; on their own path; for their own karmic progression/digression. We should try to help when we can but we cannot "change one's mind" on certain issues, etc. especially when it comes to fear. Just because others are living in fear does not mean that you need to "take that on." You live from your perspective and keep it strong (and yet open to additional changes and information). We cannot walk in another's shoes or be in their headspace as much as we want everyone to live in "love and light." It is up to each individual how they think and act. Be loving and kind and stay strong IN YOUR LIGHT connected to all that is beautiful on this planet and beyond. Take the high road, as they say, and stay in love and light while "dealing with" others. Be that love and peace you so wish to see in the world. BE IT and let your light radiate out onto the earth and all her inhabitants. That is all each of us can do to help the whole: keep our own selves "right minded" and clear and clean and loving. Just that. Let us work on self today so we can stay strong in the light. Let not other's fear blind you from your path of love. Stay strong in love.

BE the light.

And God Bless you today and all days.

TODAY'S MESSAGE

Create!

That is what we are here for (one reason). Or creation can be seen as something we have graduated to. As we become more and more connected to the one sun/son creator/life-force/greater super consciousness, we are more and more creators in that sense of the word. Let us decide what we want to create and do that. Creation can come in many forms; more than can be described here. One can create art or science or intuitive connections and events. One can create a solution to a world problem or a solution to one's own "problem." One can create their own gorgeous life aligned with Great Spirit and soar like an eagle! Let us all be ONE with creation and all that is. Let us be one with our brothers and sisters so that our creations are aligned with the greater good of all mankind. Let us love ourselves and our life-situation and let us shine that light out upon this great land (without borders). Let us be full of love for the excitement of creation: a greater good; a better world; infinite abundance (of love). Be that change you are waiting for. Create it! We are the ones we've been waiting for, as they say. BE THAT.

Blessings and Love today and ALL DAYS.

God Bless.

TODAY'S MESSAGE

We each have our gifts we bring into this worldly-experience. Are you sharing your gifts? Do you recognize them as gifts from spirit/god/creator? Are you thankful for them and enjoy sharing them? This is one thing we can do while here on planet earth: share our gifts. If everyone did this we would have a world full of beautiful happy people. However, many people are focused on other things and that is okay too. Do know that recognizing our gifts, and recognizing that we all have them, is a beautiful place to be. Another thing we do here on planet earth is to work on those other things that we've brought into this experience, and/or picked up on the way. Those negative habits and patterns that oftentimes hold us back or seem like challenges along the path. These things too can be seen as gifts as we recognize them as teachers ~ guiding us, aligning us, and showing us those things we can not only "overcome" but we can begin to understand, resolve and release. These can be past-life issues or those childhood or life traumas and/or patterning. Getting through these, and finding your way through to the other side, and gaining full-scope knowledge, is a goal we can all strive toward. Releasing these patterns and trauma help lighten our load, so to speak, so that our natural gifts can come forward with love and forever more joy: raising us each up ~ always up.

Much Love and Light To You Today and ALL Days, in ALL ways (always). LOVENLIGHT!

TODAY'S MESSAGE

So many changes happening; sometimes we feel them and other times they go unnoticed. But do know they are there and happening and all is well in the world. This world is meant for change; humankind is meant to change; you are designed to change (learn and grow). How beautiful is that? With this in mind we can "weather the storm" and not only weather the changes but be glad in it. It is important to be glad in all we do. Joy Joy Joy sounds great on some days but doesn't feel so joyous on other days. That is okay too! Do know that when you feel down, that eventually you will feel elevated. Do know (this has been said before, recently) that our moods vary and this is fine too. Not only do our moods vary but knowing that we will once again come back around to joy is very important. Lessons are being incorporated in "our system" and we move forward once again. Sometimes you may need to "rest it out" and other times run miles and skip and dance. It all depends on how you feel. It is okay to "go with how you feel" but again do know that these feelings vary. Much of it is under your control but the greater "movement" in the ups and downs is part of this cycling of life. To the cycles! Let us be happy for these for they are our teachers. Also, try to flow with the cycles too for then there is less "holding onto" the way you think it is "supposed to be." Love and light to you on this fine day.

LOVELOVELOVE! (and joy).

God Bless.

TODAY'S MESSAGE

Let us all sit for a moment and connect to our heart-space. We may first need to come back "into our bodies" for this idea to manifest. We can find the courage to really go within and this is a good place to be but may take some practice and discipline. How are you feeling? What are you thinking? How much of you is being "programmed" by the outside forces? Where is your life-force and when have you been connected to that recently? There is much in the way of programming here on planet earth. We even come into this experience with some programming and then more and more is added. We often define ourselves by how we fit into the programs that are happening each and every day around us. Do know that the truth is within and not without (on the outside). And the truth can indeed set us free. When we are connected to our hearts we are living a more authentic and loving life. When we are elsewhere we are simply following the paths programmed by others. Finding your true path and your life lessons and your purpose and/or joy, is found in your own heart. Not in the mind and not in the pain-body, but within your loving heart. That is where your love-source resides and that is where you can and should go when you are feeling "less than" and/or lacking and/or confused, in pain, etc. Do find your heart. There we gain more in the way of energy needed for our bodies and minds and even our chakras. Be in the heart as much as possible and find joy and LIVE that joy. You are amazing; go to the heart of the matter and be reminded of such.

Love and light to you on this fine day.

TODAY'S MESSAGE

There are many opportunities for growth while here on planet earth. These opportunities come in various forms. They can come "harshly" or gently. They can come from the most unlikely of people or those who constantly seem to "push your buttons." The opportunities continue to come until we realize and fully resolve certain lessons/issues. They may present themselves over and over again so that we may finally release (mind/body/spirit) certain programs or aspects of ourselves and let them go so we can finally heal. This sounds easy but often times it doesn't appear that way. Though, we can ask that it be easy. The best way for that idea to manifest is to be open for the lessons. Open for change and open for growth and open for healing: let us make that our intention today! Then we can clear up the past and move forward. Today and all days we move forward and grow with greater love in our hearts and less heaviness in our body/mind and spirit. May we all be blessed and feel the love of life today and all days, in all ways. And may your lessons be easy: let us flow with freedom grace and ease as we move forward in the light. AMEN and God/Goddess/Goodness Bless.

LOVE AND LIGHT!

TODAY'S MESSAGE

There is great love in the world and you are one. You are one with the love if you so desire. We are all one. This idea has been posed many times before and should be explored over and over again, until it is understood, for that is where we are going in our evolutionary development. We are all developing even though at times it doesn't seem that way. We are all growing and learning and evolving to become ONE with the All That Is. This is how things typically work in the universe: ONENESS that has many factors but works toward the greater good. Here on planet earth we forget about the oneness factor and it seems as if every man is out for themselves. This is a sad state of affairs but all is not lost; this is not a hopeless case. Each and every, day people put themselves out there to help their fellow man. Sacrifices are made for love (or money). It is time to move away from the materialism in the world and allow the love to rule this planet. This is an almost impossible feat but again, all hope is not lost for there are individuals each and every day working for the better good of mankind. Let that be you today. Even in the smallest of gestures we can make a difference for our own soul's growth as well as humanity at large. For even as large as our group is here on planet earth there are much greater things "out there." One need not believe in them for that to be the case. There is so much larger than us and yet again, one small gesture of kindness can save this human "race." LOVE AND LIGHT and God Bless Us: EVERY ONE.

TODAY'S MESSAGE

Life is full of surprises! Be surprised and grateful for all that
is. There is beauty here and it can show up in a variety of
ways. Just what you wish for may indeed come true so
always be open; always open. At the same time let those
things that don't fall into place go. If they were "meant to
be" they would be and if they are not (obviously) then there
is no need to panic, just let them go. It is good to have
things flowing: some things flow in and some things flow
out and as you are going WITH the flow instead of against
it, all works out accordingly. Do realize that much has to do
with timing of your path and purpose. Just because dreams
may seem to shatter doesn't mean that your life can't be
dreamy! There is so much more than that one person or that
one job or opportunity or house or car or
relationship/friendship/companion. There are SOOOOO
many things ~ why limit yourself to just that one upon
which you are so focused? A general feeling of openness for
"the highest and best good" of you and the universe helps in
that regard. Since we don't know the highest and best good
for ourselves and the universe, then an element of faith is
required. Trust that all is in divine order so the flow
continues. Be open and ready for the beauty of life and be
grateful for the surprises that enter. Let the rest go and ALL
will manifest perfectly.

God Bless and Big Love To You On This Fine Day.

TODAY'S MESSAGE

Live your life to the fullest. This has been alluded to before but what does it mean? Well, for one thing, you can live your life as YOU to the fullest or even just BE-ing that which is you and what you represent instead of hiding behind a mask so that others feel more comfortable. Toning down yourself, if you will, is another way we are not living our lives to the fullest of our nature. Letting your light shine would be the remedy. Many times we think we will not be accepted as "us" so we "tone down." Oftentimes we even tone down our "enthusiasm;" how crazy is that? Are we afraid that we would be judged simply because others don't find enthusiasm in their lives? Being happy in life is our birthright; it is truly what we are here to do. Of course we can help people and be "long suffering" but hey, if you are going to do that then you might as well be enthusiastic about it: find joy in it! Some people have gone through great struggles and have still maintained joy and enthusiasm for living: this keeps them "going" and helps them with the understanding that "it is all worth it." It IS all worth it ~ this is life ~ it is worth it so "go for it." Others have much less of a struggle in life and they have no joy at all. Their day to day is an internal struggle for them. This is sad for these people are "asleep" as their life passes them by. But this is not a place to judge, this is just the idea that some DO have great struggles and still find joy. If you find yourself struggling today, do take the time to "be" and find the beauty in all things. Others have done it and so can you. Wake up to the possibilities of living in the now and accepting life (in all its glory, as well as in the struggles, or even the mundane) LOVINGLY, OPENLY, AND WILLINGLY. BE-ing YOU to the fullest expression. Have a blessed day.

TODAY'S MESSAGE

Stay strong in the mind/body/spirit trinity and all is well.
There is great fear-based programming in the country these
days and the best way to move away from living in fear, and
living IN LOVE, is to strengthen your system. This can be
done with meditation, yoga, loving/kindness, and self-care.
We often forget self-care during times of stress and dealing
with "issues," but as has been said before, each of us cannot
help another or perform at our best, without self-care. All of
this (meditation and yoga and prayer and self-care) is not just
for you, it is for the planet. For as you improve and
maintain YOU, the better for the planet as a whole. Release
YOUR judgment; find YOUR heart; be in LOVE WITH
YOU AND YOUR LIFE, and all will be fine. If and when
your thoughts dip below that of enthusiasm and joy, please
do work on self and find that joy within. Living from joy
and love is a great place to be. Sometimes we think we don't
deserve this while others are suffering but I assure you the
best way to help others in suffering, and help the
WHOLENESS OF ONENESS is to help thyself. Then you
can share it with others. If you have it not, there is nothing
to share. It is as easy as that. Stay strong in your trinity of
mind/body/spirit by clearing the energy centers, the chakras.
Take time to clear your auric field and where you live and
work and play. All is helpful in this regard. Stay strong for
you are the light of the world. Strengthen it and shine it out
for all who needs it (and many need it today). Kindness and
compassion comes from your heart and a clear mind. Hence
the self-care to get you prepared. LOVENLIGHT and have
a wonder-filled day.

TODAY'S MESSAGE

When we find the gift in the littlest of things, we find beauty in living this most sacred life. There are great miracles here, as has been said before, but when our eyes and hearts are focused on other things, we miss them! Miracles are often subtle and finding miracles takes practice; and patience. Finding miracles takes an openness to the awareness of the highest of light. There is much light here on planet earth ~ most people are simply being distracted, so they don't see it. Many focus on "the negative." Have you ever thought there may be miracles in that what we consider negative, as well? Practicing and finding the miracles in all things is a great way to go about your day. At the same time, do be aware there is much negative program happening "within the system," right now. Finding miracles can help dispel some of those effects and at the same time we may wish to stay practiced in our clearing, centering and grounding. It is up to us to focus on our prime light maintenance. We cannot find it from the outside so practice it from the inside today. Keep yourself as clear as possible, free from the fear and programming, connected to your heart. Breathe in and out and concentrate on the breath when you begin to feel lost. All is perfect here. There are miracles happening, even within the "negative events." Stay strong in the light and keep breathing and clearing! Keep loving and laughing.

YOU are a miracle so stay loving and perfect.

Blessed Be.

Blessed Be.

TODAY'S MESSAGE

Tap into the glory of the All That Is. Go there and BE
THAT. There really is this place of higher thinking and
being and living and it is right here for you. Most of the
time we are stuck in this low-base thinking, acting and being.
It is heavy here on planet earth and many find it "hard" to
be here. Sometimes people tap into the All That Is and are
so happy there, and then they forget or are forced back into
lower based heavy thinking and they become saddened or
depressed. All you need to do is remember to elevate
yourself back up there where you belong. One can be in the
All That Is higher based thinking, acting and being and
experience the same "mundane" existence as their fellow
man, but see it in a totally different light. One can see life
through the eyes of love and enjoy (live in-joy). With a
feeling of a "higher calling" and a divine presence in all
things, one's life can change for the better. We are all here
to experience. We can all be experiencing much of the same
things. However, it is the way one paints their picture as to
how beautiful their canvas becomes. There is much beauty
here so don't forget to paint your picture of life using all the
radiant colors of the central sun/son. Knowing that all
colors (sounds, words, visions, experiences) are special and
unique, we can lessen the duality-judgment and simply dance
in the light. There is much light around and as has been said
before, if you cannot find this light and cannot see it, then
simply tap into your heart-space to BE it. Shine it out to the
world and brighten their day. Enjoy all moments for all are
sacred on your canvas. Clean up your canvas too so that the
colors shine pure in the glory of oneness. God Bless and
Have a Super Day!

TODAY'S MESSAGE

Every day is perfect for every day is a new opportunity for a new you and a new life and a new perspective on your life that can make your day AMAZING! Life is so beautiful when we are grateful for all that is. Life is so amazing and miraculous when we go with the flow of the universe of unlimited abundance! And what do we do with all of this abundance? Well, a good thing to do would be to share it. Learning to share and be a part of the Great I AM is a beautiful place to be. Learning to love others unconditionally (without thinking of "a return") is something we all are learning ~ whether we ask for this or not ~ it is where this planet is "going." We need to go there: we need to understand unconditional love for this is the earth's intention too. As ONE we must "get this idea" in order to evolve to higher levels of consciousness and the universe and our earth are all rooting for this: that soon we eventually get this idea and start implementing it on a day to day basis. When we all live with unconditional love then there is no greed or anger or jealousy. This may be why you are gaining such lessons ~ so that you get closer and closer to living a life of unconditional love. LOVE is something that many people struggle with. There is no struggle when love is unconditional for then and only then is love working in its purest form. Only then is it "true love." May you love yourself unconditionally and may you love the earth and sky in that manner. And with each and every communication and interaction ~ may it be through love. AMEN! LOVE AND LIGHT TO YOU ON THIS FINE DAY.
BLESSINGS ~

TODAY'S MESSAGE

Do know that emotions and feelings change. Just because you feel you can't make it through one more moment of today doesn't mean you won't be "over the moon" tomorrow. The idea here is to "push through" and experience your emotions to clear up old patterns so that one day eventually these issues won't "push you around" any longer. One needs to go through these emotions and experience them fully, loving and willingly before one can "move on" so they effect you no longer. Also know that as uncomfortable as you may be "going through it" the clearer you may eventually be when you get to the other side. People often don't like to feel uncomfortable and people too don't like to "work" at things (like "their stuff) but again the idea here is to push through and know that when you get through to the other side you will feel so much better. Then those demons that once haunted you will no longer be triggers ~ so it is worth the "work." It is NOT worth avoiding and numbing these problems. Yes, sometimes you can just lay there and cry it out or wallow in your sorrow: THAT is still much healthier than avoidance. Your body and mind and spirit remember the "issues" regardless of the fact that you may not wish to reflect on them. They are still there. So do know that you are very much loved from the higher realms and that ALL YOU DO is worth it for you are learning and growing and breaking the old karmic patterns. The work is worth it; you are worth it. EVERYTHING is temporary; your emotions and feelings and what you are "going through" is temporary. So do keep trying: loving, forgiving (of others as well as SELF) and BE-ing that perfectly awesome person you are right now. Do give yourself an energy hug today: **FOR YOU ARE LOVED!**

TODAY'S MESSAGE

We are perfect just the way we are. Right here, right now, everything is perfect. Sometimes we feel we are not enough and that the world needs to change and we need to change and all is "going to hell in a hand-basket." That is fine. We can work with those ideas. Let us first work with self and getting self "on track" to feeling at one with the universe. Combining the trinity (body, mind and spirit) is a good place to start. Our minds may be going in one direction where our bodies feel something different and our spirit has a "bigger plan." STOP. Just close your eyes and breathe. Come to your heart-center and breathe there. Just imagine you're breathing in and out of your "high heart." Notice the body calm down. Notice the thoughts calm down. If they don't, then perfect: just keep breathing. Allow the thoughts to come and go ~ maybe there is some processing that needs to take place there. Notice the "negative pattern thinking" that occurs in your thoughts. Turn them around with beautiful words to self. Give self-affirmations of loving kindness as you would to a stranger in need. You are perfect. Life is beautiful. You are beautiful. You are enough. This moment is enough. Keep breathing and let go of "all that does not serve you." Ask for this internally ~ for all that does not serve you to leave your mind/body/spirit system. Breathe and repeat as often as necessary until you feel an ease. Ask for the integration of the systems: body, mind and spirit. Ask for protection after clearing the energy in and around you. Be brave. Remind yourself how brave you are. And strong: believe it! Keep breathing and you will eventually live it. Regardless, all is perfect, as are you. The above may just help remind you of this fact. **You are perfect.**

TODAY'S MESSAGE

Everything is beautiful here on planet earth. It is all based on perception. Sometimes we have fear and our perception is coated with the idea that things are out to harm us. Sometimes we have joy and have you noticed how that idea ~ of things out to harm us ~ fades away when we are in this light? You don't even think of it for you are in another perception of life. THIS is the beauty of getting one's perception lined up with how one wishes to live in this world. If you want to live in peace then your perception should be coming from a peaceful place ~ it starts with you and your own mind, see? So we can come from a place of love or come from a place of peace, or come from a place or torment and fear and the "why me" idea (a very common debate). Live from whatever perception you would like and that is now your world. BUT if you really want that peace you so care about, and that love you so need, and that happiness you desperately search for, then come from peace and love and happiness. It starts with you: your own mind and your own heart. Do know this is not just "word play" this is an elemental truth: for "like attracts like." So what are you "liking" today? Instead of the "poor me" how about you change that to "fantastic and amazing me!" and see how things turn around for you. GRATITUDE, LOVE, FORGIVENESS AND OPENNESS are pivotal to the evolution of your soul and that of the planet (yeah, just that). You've got this! Sometimes we just need to be reminded.

ALL adds up to new understandings ~ just stay open and proceed forward!

TODAY'S MESSAGE

So much to do here on planet earth! How are you enjoying the experience? Sometimes we feel we are just coping; other times we feel we are flying high. This is fine for this is life. Do know that being in the flow of life and the flow of the universe is a good place to be. This has been said before but is a good reminder. Do know that you can manifest whatever you wish: so stick with it! However, being in the flow of the universe helps the universe better provide for you (again, this has been said before but worth repeating). How to do? How to do? Just "let it go," as they say. Yes, easier said than done but do know if we TRUST and we continue on (or sometimes just take a pause; take a nap) then things do follow through when it comes to our needs, our growth, and our evolution. You need not get angry with the universe and shake your fist! That probably won't help much. But the idea of GRATITUDE ~ now that will help greatly. Then you are in the flow and are grateful then you are in touch with what is really important: your heart, your growth; your love-factor. BE the love and it will gravitate toward you. BE faithful and many surprises will continue your way.

Life if funny: laugh at it all and proceed ahead!

That is key!

And do so with love; always with LOVE.

TODAY'S MESSAGE

There are many experiences we can have here on planet earth. Experiencing things consciously, fully, and with the heart open, is a good way to be. Much of the time we live with our eyes cast down and not really opening to each experience. Sometimes that may be because we are "working" or those times seem "mundane." Though every experience can be extraordinary if we are open to it ALL. There is greatness here! This is the place to be, right here in this experience, as the world changes and you change with it. This may sometimes feel constricting or "crazy making" but this life, your life, right here and now is exceptional and an OPPORTUNITY for you and all men to evolve and become better: more loving, more open-hearted, and more ONE with the universe. It is time to become one with humanity (regardless of race or creed). It is time to become one with all the other creatures that share our planet as well. It is time to become one with the rest of the universe that pulses and thrives and is little noticed by most humans living here on earth. THIS is the time and you are the ONE! Be open; be loving. Learn your lessons so you can grow and evolve and be happy in it. Then, the whole world becomes lighter and brighter and the universe sings . . . all because of YOU and your good (light) work.

God Bless and have a great day.

TODAY'S MESSAGE

We are each and every one of us, here on planet earth, truly blessed. We have the beauty of the planet and the relationships with other souls: human and animal and all the rest. We have people that "resonate" with us and those who seem foreign. We have all we need here to flourish. We have all we need here to learn lessons and to live our life's purpose. But many here are struggling; they don't like it here. It is not that they are not awake, sometimes they are: they just don't like all the heaviness; the negativity. More people, than not, are here and seem "attached" to being here; they run the gamut of emotions and focus on the day to day things that aren't "super important." Sometimes they are so focused on these things they don't even think of "soul purpose" and "life lessons." Can you imagine? That is fine. There will be opportunities that will come into their experience for them to remember this idea. Or they may simply need to work on these things at another time, another place, when they are not so focused on the basics of the human experience: sex, money, fame. There are many words that people could substitute there ~ it all has to do with focus/perception and the inability to be open/awake. Do take the time today to be open and awake and focused on LOVE and LIGHT. Those are wonderful things upon which to focus. While you are at it, try to release some of the pressure you put on yourself when it comes to life lessons and purpose. It is better to just BE in the experience and allow those things to become manifest. YOU just BE. Be open; be brave: be LOVE! God Bless and have a great day!

TODAY'S MESSAGE

There are so many levels in which we live. We are not conscious of all the levels for that would be too much to "handle." We come into this world to accomplish certain things, to remedy old karmic patterns, to live our "purpose." This can take many forms that may seem outside our selves but in reality, it is all within. This idea of life being "within you" has been said so many times before but this idea now is one that all the many levels and realms are still within each one of us, as well. Do know that all may not make sense; that things may seem like it has no purpose; that your life doesn't seem to change that much despite all your work and learning of lessons, etc. It is all perfect for we don't know it ALL and the point here is that there is a lot of the ALL out there, affecting us: more than we could ever imagine. Know one thing, though. Do know that you are loved. Do know that the ALL-THAT-IS, is loving, and has your best interest "at heart." Do know you are perfect where you are right now and if you do absolutely nothing else while here on planet earth you are still SUPER AWESOME! Love is like that. Life is like that. We are one and you are doing a great job. Keep up the good lightwork and do be reminded each and every moment of every day that the higher realms love you and that your life is unfolding in a divine manner (despite appearances to the contrary).

Feel blessed because you are.

All is well and you are PERFECT!

TODAY'S MESSAGE

Love is Light, and Light is Love, and you are Gorgeous! We could stop right there: if you believed it. But most people don't "own up" to their grandeur. Most people don't shine their light all of the time. Most people don't believe (truly in their true-heart-space) that love can heal the world. Most people just get discouraged with how things "are" here on planet earth. Sometimes happy; sometimes sad; rarely fully present; rarely shining their heart-light. That is fine for that is how things roll here on planet earth. But some day we will all shine in our brightness and our glory. Some day we will be joyous and full of knowledge (knowing/feeling/gratitude). Some day we will love each other and especially love ourselves. We will understand the nature of our "challenges" and work our way through them. Someday soon we will understand the dynamics of peace as well as the "strife" that may be required to take us there. Life is full of wonder. Do find wonder in the experience. Be bright and shiny. Be happy and joyous. Today may be the day you "see" that you are gorgeous: that you are light. Today may be the day that your loving heart heals the world; heals YOUR sadness and fear.

Be BRAVE today and walk in love.

LOVENLIGHT and have a Blessed Day.

TODAY'S MESSAGE

There are great things in you just dying to be unleashed on the world! Are you covering up some of your greatness? You may not realize it but at times you may be hiding some of your light. Do you feel others won't understand you so you diminish yourself? That is a sad thing but also a very common occurrence here on planet earth. Of course we want to work with others and meet people "where they are," but that does not mean you need to lessen your splendor NOR YOUR JOY. Do find that you, that higher/glorious/victorious you, that is hiding within and allow it to flourish. Do allow yourself to experience unlimited joy. There is great potential in you and no man can limit you ~ only you can do that. This may be done unconsciously so as we begin to be more and more aware we can be more and more aware of our light and how we yield it. This is a time to release the light for the world to see. This is a time to be BRAVE! You and your beautiful soul have every right to be joyful and happy as often as you can find it in yourself to let go and allow that to happen. Now is not the time to hide; now is the time to shine!

Do be brave and step into your light;

today and every day.

God Bless; now and always (all-ways).

TODAY'S MESSAGE

Where ever you are ~ BE in that moment. If you are feeling
down you can go in and look at it. You can even cry a
thousand tears and release it. If you are feeling up then be
IN the "up" and be grounded in it too. If you are in-
between then BE there. The idea is to stop avoiding and to
really be a part of your life. This seems funny when you
think about it: how much we try to avoid our actual lives
and the living of such. This can happen in sickness and
when we avoid being fully present during things we don't
particularly enjoy (traffic, work, etc.). Let us take the time to
invest ourselves and BE in our bodies and feel the
experience of all we do. Instead of "tuning out" ~ let's
"tune in" ~ as they once said repeatedly in the 60's. Now is
a time to be fully present for now is a time where many
energies are swirling around and we want to be more "in our
bodies" so we don't "loose our marbles," if you will. It is
easy to blow our tops, is the idea here, BUT if we are really
HERE in the now, the chance for that happening is much
less. Another idea relating to this would be less multi-tasking
and more focusing on the job at hand (or the
communication, the relating, the living). This may seem like
it will slow you down but it will better keep you focused and
on-track so do try to notice this today as well. Less tuning
out and less multi-tasking and less doing all those things we
do to find escape. Why escape this? This is your life? LIVE
IT FULLY and with so much love in your heart and
gratitude for the experience. GOOD LUCK!

And have a Blessed Day. LOVENLIGHT!

TODAY'S MESSAGE

We are all part and parcel of the Great I AM. Are you living and working and BE-ing in the Greatness? This is a good place to be but sometimes hard to find and maintain. There is much happening on planet earth that takes us away from our loving-light selves and when that happens we move away from the inner knowing and the super-conscious-all-knowing, and move into fear and anger and irritation and self-focus-blame. Moreover we blame others for our "misfortunes." Let us take today to get "back on track" to find ourselves once again, and to be, and work, and live, in LOVE. This sounds easy and can be easy. It only takes a switch in perception and intention and then again here we are in the great ever-presence. The idea is to get reconnected! We lose our connection every time we go to the intellect and try to work things out there. Moreover, it is in that space where we often ruminate on the "poor me" idea and that too takes us away from the connection to source. If you have complaints and concerns, then take them to the source and leave them there. Ask for explanation as well as a new understanding or knowing about particular situations. Ask for these situations to be released from the mind-chatter and directed, energetically, out of the body system. These are nice tools to clear our mind/body/spirit so do use them. Even if you don't 100% believe they would work, try it, and you may see that you feel better and then your belief grows as well (and that is always a good thing). Keep coming back to your heart-space when you find yourself scattered. The earth energy is in flux and this takes its toll on our "vessels" but a little maintenance can get us back into the flow of the Great I AM. Say it: Almighty I AM; Almighty I AM; Almighty I AM!

TODAY'S MESSAGE

Don't give up hope!

There is much good here on planet earth. Look around with eyes of love and you will see it! Don't lose faith. Faith is a strong indicator of what will be. Strengthen your faith by looking around with eyes of love and seeing all the beauty in the world. You will not find it on your phones, computers, internet, or the evening news. Beauty is in your heart and in your fellow brethren. Keep the idea of beauty and oneness strengthened within so that beauty and oneness can be created without (on the outer experience). We are what we think so your thoughts are important. Your dreams of a new beautiful tomorrow is important. Find the beauty: it is there; it is here! Find it and nourish it and allow it to grow deeply and then expand it out unto the world. We are beautiful despite our faults. The world is beautiful despite the turbulence. Life is beautiful despite the pain. Keep faith. Stay strong. Breathe deep. Meditation helps you find the beauty: go there. Loving others helps you find the beauty: do that. Hug your pet; hug a tree; sing your song. See the beauty? Yes, it is here. You are here. Let us all make the best of it during these transitional times. All is well. Life is perfect, as are you.

Love and Light and Many Blessings from Above.

God Bless.

TODAY'S MESSAGE

Find peace within. Do look within for the peace and allow the fear to dissipate. That fear is coming from external factors and you need not look there for your peace. Go within instead. You will know things better there. You will be able to grasp the bigger picture as you tap into the super conscious love light of all that is; of the god/good source; of the light. We can easily become frightened by the news, the media, and all the negativity flying here and there. This fear mongering is infiltrated on the internet and the television shows and even through communication with others. Is that where you want to be? Is that how you want to live? No, you want to live in peace and that peace is in your heart and your true-life-being. This is not to say to turn a blind-eye. This is to say, go within to find truth for yourself and the world-as-is. As you practice meditation and prayer and vigilance in your practice of clearing and centering, you will find that the fear goes away. Fear is False Evidence Appearing Real. Do note the differences between that and where you are right now (not the future, but here and now). Are you safe and secure? Meditate and breathe and you will find that you are. All is one and you are just fine. Practice, practice, practice what you know when it comes to clearing and grounding. Find the peace; go there. It helps you and it helps the world at large. BE and all will BE fine. LOVENLIGHT! And have a Blessed Day ~ without the fear by finding the peace within.

AMEN!

TODAY'S MESSAGE

Here we are: living breathing entities. We are multi-faceted individuals and the various dynamics combine to create one person: spiritual, physical, mental, energetic beings. This is spectacular! And then the individuals come together and create families and friends and tribes. Together they become communities, towns, cities and countries and then of course the world planet of inhabitants. We can go micro with this and we can go macro. More and more we can understand that it takes the individual parts to make up the whole and that there is always more and more: above and beyond, or deeper and more refined. But together is where it's at, for as we combine, we change and grow and morph into "the more." Don't turn away from the "all that is." Jump into it instead. Hug and love all around you and allow your "vibe" to permeate that which is in your experience. Send your love-vibe out even further and encapsulate your family and friends. And then further out still to your tribe and communities. And then further still until you reach all around the world. Don't forget the animals and plants, the insects and the trees: macro to the micro and then visa-versa. Remember the love to self, encasing you and your aura field and then deeper within to each and every cell. Life is amazing and so are you! Keep the love up up up as we go "higher vibrational." And do be kind; for we all need more kindness and understanding in the world today.

LOVENLIGHT and have a great day.

BLESSINGS ~

TODAY'S MESSAGE

We know not the thoughts, nor the motivations, of others.
We don't know their fears or their path. We don't know! So
why do we take on the energies of those who are "acting
out" around us? Why would we assume anything? Though
we are human, so this is what we do. During these
situations, it is good to notice OUR reaction to any given
situation and learn from THERE. It is all about SELF and
how we can release, learn and grown. No judgment on the
other; let us worry about ourselves instead. Sometimes we
may be confronted by dangerous or obnoxious (toxic)
people and situations. And from there create great growth
spurts in our own experience/existence. We should almost
THANK those people who've created such a rift in our
energy system. This rift is an opening. This opening is the
impetus of evolution, motivation and change. The earth
goes through great changes in a similar manner with
earthquakes and volcanos; a change in the weather. These
changes create newness of being. From the fire, the wind,
and the water, the planet changes, forms and grows. You
too form by the force of all creation. Sometimes it takes
such power to create change. Enjoy this process and be easy
on yourself as well as those others who may seem to be
"bothering" you. They may be there to help create beautiful
changes within you. So thank them and be grateful of all
that is.

Blessings to you on this fine day.

LOVENLIGHT!

TODAY'S MESSAGE

Love is all around for the taking.

There is great love here on planet earth. Open to it and
there it shall be. Of course there are certain places on earth
on any given day/minute/second where bad things happen
and there is sickness, disease, death and war. These places
too can still be full of love. Love can be within and bathed
around EVERY circumstance: all of them. We are born
and we die and we are born again. We can be born again in
this physical life too simply by opening the eyes and heart
and CHANGING perspective. As we live in love and peace
and harmony ~ if you really "go there" fully and with total
belief and resolve ~ then you will find that LOVE and
PEACE will be yours. As within you find; so you will find
on your outside experiences ~ see? This is how things work
for "like attracts like," so they say. Here is a prime example.
What you have within will be attracted to you. What you
focus on increases. Why would you not want to focus upon
peace and love in your heart right now and amplify your
experiences here on earth to be one of radiance and light;
love and joy?

This too can be yours.

It all starts within you.

Blessings, Love and Light now and forever.

AMEN!

TODAY'S MESSAGE

Life is beautiful when you allow the flow of grace to ease in
and out of your interactions and experience. Living in the
flow of grace lets you drop the expectations and find
enjoyment in the natural connections that are found here on
earth. Let us look at the connections we can enjoy each and
every day. All can be made fun and lighthearted. Slowing it
down and really coming into the presence of the moment.
This is beautiful; as are you. Life is beautiful. There is great
joy here ~ don't miss it! Watch your thoughts for if they are
a constant worry and a feeling of resentment or fear then
simply stop and "smell the roses" as they say. Your time is
now here on earth; the moment here and now is where we
live, we shine and we experience. If we are always worried
about what we are missing then we will miss the beauty that
occurs naturally in living each and every second of every day.
We are all one and you are glorious. The better and more
"shiny" we make ourselves, the more the brilliance of this
earth can resound through the universe. As a one living
breathing ball of joy!

Enjoy.

You deserve it.

Now is the only time; right now: find joy.

It helps you; it helps the world.

Namaste'

TODAY'S MESSAGE

Deep breath. And again, another. Do think of grounding and breath-work during these changing times. Do work on self and PUSH THROUGH any of the old programs and obstacles that no longer serve you. This is a time to do self-work and find that clear-core-you. We can stop it all and hide under the rug OR WE CAN STEP UP AND SAY YES, LET'S DO THIS ~ I AM READY! That is a good way to be; not buying into the old ways and what other people (society/media) is telling you how life should be, but more YOU finding that REAL YOU and embracing him or her and saying I LOVE YOU and I LOVE LIFE and I WILL HONOR ALL THAT IS AND BE – BE ME! Just BE to the fullest expression ~ this is funny for THAT is not an easy task. It is kind of easy because if and when we say, YES LET'S DO THIS, and at the same time release all the old muck and mire of the everyman's-world, then there it is, and there you are, and now you can BE for that is what remains. First one must let go of all the self-judgments and all the ideas of things being "unfair." It is easy to blame one's misfortunes on others. It is admirable when one pushes through. It is beautiful being on "the other side" of those barriers we place on ourselves. It just takes a little work and some reflection. Take a deep breath and find your center-balance. Then let the rest go.

Breathe; breathe; breathe.

ENJOY!

IN – JOY.

TODAY'S MESSAGE

Do breathe deep and do slow down. There is all the time
you need to get things done and despite what circulates on
the news and despite what may even present itself in your
physical reality ~ IT (as well as you) is all perfect. This is life
on planet earth and we are in for many changes. Change is
always happening but sometimes it is slow and flowing
changes and other times it seems quick, sharp and abrupt.
That is how life is here, again; this is life on planet earth ~
there are cycles and rhythms and some feel harsh. Though
things change HERE one thing stays consistent and that is
your soul/spirit/love self. That is STRONG and is there for
you when you connect to it; when you remember who you
ARE and reconnect THERE. This everlasting-soul-self-you
knows that all is perfect and has a greater more broad view
than us mere mortals. Trust it; go there. The soul-self-you
is connected with all that is and is wise and knows what you
want and what you need. It is there to reassure you that you
HAVE all you need and that the only thing you DON'T
need is a fearful mind. Move away from the fear and find
your center. Take the deep breaths you practice and ground
yourself. You are fine; you are whole within; you need
nothing from the outside. Go to the heart –center as often
as possible. Stop RE-acting and get centered. Only then will
you be back in the flow of life; without the fear and torture
we often allow to creep in to our existence. Breathe deep
and have faith.

LOVEANDLIGHT.

God Bless.

TODAY'S MESSAGE

All is one. You are one with the universe and we are each whole. Meaning ~ we have all we need for we are one with the universe and one with all around us. Do open up to the idea of oneness and how we live and breathe together on this earth; with this earth mother goddess Gaia. She is living and breathing just like you. She needs the love and affection of your warm hearts and gentle spirit. She is tired of all the fighting and to know that YOU love her and that YOU send her warm earth-hugs, is a beautiful thing. One person cannot fix all that has happened on this earth. The earth has seen many battles and has endured many scars and faced much neglect and sabotage. Simple greed and disregard of all that is living is usually where this stems from and of course it is not your doing. The idea of an apology to the mother is a good idea and an apology to the father sun god and an apology to all living beings here on planet earth is a good idea. This isn't you taking on the responsibility but just you acknowledging the great respect that we have here for all living things for so many people don't even think of this. Many people are quite self-focused. And yet others are absorbing "all the negative" and taking it on themselves which too is not a good thing for how can you shine when you are so loaded down with grief. Do take time today to love thy brothers and sisters and thy mother and father. Do love yourself . . . don't forget your own heart-soul that needs love. There is much to go around and as you give so you receive. All is well; all is one; you are perfect and have all you need. God Bless

TODAY'S MESSAGE

You can't do everything in a day but you can be present during everything you do in a day, see? This is the idea to let go of "must do" and concentrate on being present. Much of the time when we go about the day thinking we "must do" then our doing becomes a chore. Isn't it much better when our day is full or rainbows and blessings? Do allow the universe to help bring things into your awareness and reality. Do allow help from others for people so love to help. Ask for what you need and be ready for answers and gifts. Giving to others is also a good way to manifest beauty in your own life for as the old adage goes, to give is to receive. Don't hold back on the love one can give to the world; you have so much beauty and light and as we let go of the resistances to be and give and love with joy, then again, more and more joy and love and giving will become manifest in your own life. This isn't fantasy; this is the way of the universe. There is much joy here: find it and share it. All is not lost on planet earth. Much is changing and yes some news seems grim but you know you are strong and beautiful and it is all worth it. Hang in there for it is all so perfect; as are you.

God bless!

LOVEANDLIGHT!

And spread that joy around for more and more joy will increase within you as you do.

TODAY'S MESSAGE

Now is the time to be the best! Be the best you can be and be present in your best-ness. One need not take the weight of the world on their shoulders; instead, be the best you can be. Many feel the pain of others and it "gets them down" and they forget who they are! They are divine beings. You are a divine being waiting to blossom ~ to emerge from the chrysalis and fly, fly, fly. We are all moving up. Regardless of what appears on television and the media ~ we are finding our wings. Each is on their own path so stay focused on YOUR path. Help thy brothers and sisters, yes, but stay strong in self! Love is the key here and one must find that loving heart that is within. It is there, though possibly under much of the muck and mire of this "real world." But the greatest of worlds is within thy own heart. Go there! When you are feeling lost or confused, go there. We all have things we need to "deal with" but staying strong in loving-heart-self will help us all find our home: our heaven on earth. As has been said before ~ you cannot find that from another ~ but only from within. Go there to be your best self. Go there to be full of love and light. Seek it not on the outside but within. Within. You are a divine spirit-soul of love and light and you will recognize yourself within.

Others will not show this to you ~ it is up to you to show it to yourself.

GOD BLESS!

TODAY'S MESSAGE

All happens in divine timing. Sometimes we push things to happen or regret when things don't happen at a certain time and much of this can be relieved as we begin to step more and more "in the flow." There is much love and light here on planet earth and a super conscious filled with unlimited possibilities. Line up your intentions and stand in your power and yet let go just a bit on the "W"s: the when, where and how-for. Let go and feel the flow of life ~ that is where the action is ~ that is where our wishes and intentions become manifest. When we stand and dance and laugh from a "love space" then there is much less resistance around all aspects of our life and therefore more blessings and love come our way. It feels uncomfortable for most to go with the flow and fully step into the divine presence. That is fine. When the timing is right, there you will be! There is some practice though that can take place to help get you there quicker: release, release, release! Release all your expectations on how life should be for you and release all those troubling times when you feel you've been slighted. LET IT GO! Now is the time for divine manifestation. Now is the time to BE THE LIGHT. Now is the time for love to flow. And there you are; and there you shall be. For it is all in divine timing . . .

BE THE LOVE; BE THE LIGHT AND GOD BLESS.

NOW AND ALL DAYS.

TODAY'S MESSAGE

Where is your faith? Where is your faith in mankind, in yourself, in a higher power? This is a good time to work on faith and our own core power of strength and resolve. It takes a lot to stay in peace when the world appears threatening. It takes a lot to stay in peace when you feel threatened by others. Many of us cause quite a disturbance in our own fields and we almost threaten ourselves, through our own thoughts, if we forget to stay diligent. Diligently peaceful and bright with the idea that it is all "worth it." This is not a test and yet we can work on it like it is. Life is life and it is VERY IMPORTANT. Each action is important and each thought and feeling. It reverberates out into the world and the universe and beyond! Have you ever thought of that? So that is why we should stay diligent in our peace-practice and work on self-love and resolve. The idea that we can practice living "as a test" can take place each and every second of every day by looking upon what you are "reacting" to and how you feel within. Just breathe into it and you will know that life is okay. It is not only okay ~ each breath is a gift ~ and when you close your eyes and feel deep down in your heart you will remember. So for today let us practice peace like it is a test. Notice the reactions and feelings and sometimes you just may need to stop yourself and breathe. Rebalance FIRST and then move forward; each step lighting the way for the better. A life full of hope; a life full of love; a world full of peace is ours to behold.

Keep the faith!

And so it is.

TODAY'S MESSAGE

Make the best of your time here on planet earth. Make the best of the day, this hour; this minute. Each second is a gift and the more we smile and laugh and sing the more we will feel that this is indeed the case. A gift for you ~ this breath, this air; the water, the earth, the plants and trees. Mother Nature sings about these gifts in the winds and the rain and the sun, and we too can join her in song. Sometimes it is a strong beat and sometimes we are barely breathing but regardless we can appreciate each moment. Truly open to gratitude and love at each and every turn on your path. This life is not what it seems and we won't ever know its full/true meaning. But we can revel in the ideas! We can be curious of the process! We can be kind and loving during the adventure and grow and learn and be free. Don't let the weight of the world weigh you down. There is too much beauty here. Turn off the ideas of wrong-doing and right-doing and as Rumi once versed: there is a field ~ I will meet you there. That place is in your heart. That place is in your love-light. That place is within you! Do enjoy it and let it shine out to the world.

God/Good/Goddess Bless.

Forever and ever.

AMEN!

TODAY'S MESSAGE

Be ready for anything! That is not a threat nor is it a treat
but more like a simple opening for whatever may be
available for you at any given time. Do know our thoughts
are super important these days and that to keep ourselves
"straight" is a good way to be. Many may wish to "zone-
out" these days or use old habits to get through the day but
to do so one would miss out on all the wonderful things the
universe can provide for us at any given time. For as we are
hiding under our beds with our hands over our heads the
universe cannot an opening for all your great manifestations!
So stay open and as cheerful as possible. There is much in
the way of fear coming out through our societal programs
and within our individual programs and patterns. This has
been said before. That is okay: just recognize! Just allow
things to flow but you stay strong in your flow through love
and light projects, thoughts, words, deeds. This is easier said
than done but now is a great time to practice. Discipline in
thoughts and actions and using one's tools to help not only
manifest your day/moment but also really using the clearing
tools as well. Let us take simple steps first: chakra clearing,
meditation, yoga. If that is too difficult to ask then find
something, anything, that uplifts you. Know that things
change quickly so as you are working with your tools, still be
open for the greatness of the oneness of all creation. We are
here for you and you are doing a stellar job. Keep up the
good (light) work. AND SMILE for heaven's sake . . . that
is always a positive step in the right direction!

LOVEANDLIGHT!

TODAY'S MESSAGE

We are all here together on planet earth and yet we feel
separate and alone. We side up with different groups and
find ourselves hating other groups. We look with judgment
on others and the world and we get more angry and
frustrated each and every day. Groups blame other groups
for their misfortune and rage. That's what happens here on
planet earth. And yet, there is great kindness-learning
happening here on earth; despite the rage there are those
who are growing and awakening to the love energy: the
energy of source; the belief in the wholeness of oneness.
Religion does not define you; race and sex do not define you:
the differences finding themselves here on planet earth at
this time are the differences between those who love and
those who live in fear. The fear creates the rest of the mess:
war, anger, hatred and more; unfortunately so much more.
At the same time these occurrences of outrage, if you will,
trigger more people to awaken and open up and ask for a
better way. All one needs to do is open their hearts and the
way is made known to them. How beautiful is that? Fear
not the ways of the world. Focus on your world ~ that inner
awareness ~ and make that the best home it can be. Full of
love and light and more will follow. Stay true to your path
and more will be revealed. For now just love, release the
fear, and let go/god/source/oneness. It is easier said than
done but I know you are up to the task! Stay on the path of
love and have a blessed day.

LOVEANDLIGHT!

TODAY'S MESSAGE

We are ONE! Congratulations and celebrations are in order!
When this world (or a good portion of such) realizes this
idea there will be peace on earth. Stand up for the
ONENESS of mankind; let no man-made thinking divide
us; put us/this concept asunder. For we need the unity right
now. We need to feel the one-heart-beat of earth and all her
inhabitants. This is a sound of the divine spirit pulsing
through our veins, so to speak; beating our heart, warming
our souls, nourishing our collective spirit. Without THE
ONE we are nothing. We feel we are important when we
have strength in independence but the strength actually lies
in the collective whole. How can we get others to learn this?
We BE the oneness; we find our soul purpose and resonate
there and work toward the betterment of mankind; we smile
at EVERYONE and shine the love and light of the creator
that is radiating through us out to the masses (or whoever
you might happen to run into today). We, as an individual,
can do much in the way of generating more and more love
energy to the wholeness of oneness. However, don't beat
yourself up if you feel like you've fallen short in a
communication or interaction with another. Send love and
healing light to that person and move on. Touch more and
more people and stay strong in your power of holiness. We
are all holy for we come from the source. All are holy; they
just forgot. Remind them today with a smile, a kiss, a wave
of the hand or just your simple light radiating from all you
do. God Bless and thank you for being here today.

YOU ARE NEEDED; YOU ARE IMPORTANT.

TODAY'S MESSAGE

Life is magical; as are you. Life is full of beauty and
surprises. Are you showing up for all that is? It is good to
be open to the magic of living and be happy in it. This is
hard to do sometimes as we work and play and communicate
with others but in all that we do it would be super wonderful
to be open and excited as well as loving in honor of yourself
here on planet earth at this time and the twisting and twirling
energy of change. Many are fearful these days. Others are
ecstatic. Others are sporadic and relatively disjointed. All is
well for we are all on different paths: different paths of
awareness and different perspectives and different
vibrational developmental planes; its fine to be this way. The
universe works that way as well: in layers; in different
dimensions: some more dense than others; some more
difficult than others; some taking more "time" than others.
That is why it is good to be relatively open to all things for
we know not all that is. We will never know it all in words.
We may know it one day in our hearts and in our
being(ness). Some know much as they tap into the source:
the super conscious. But putting it all down (or out) in
words is most impossible and really, there is so much that
would not be understood anyway that it is kind of a waste of
time. But we get bits and pieces here and there and we
become more knowledgeable and aware and we build from
that knowledge and gain more and more, reaching higher;
always higher. For today, let us just be open to the loving
light of the universe and swim in the tides and the waves of
awareness. It is there for every man who awakens to it.
Have a Beautiful Day of Magic, Laughter and Joy.

TODAY'S MESSAGE

Today is like all days and yet today is unique. Now is unique; now is the time. Be in this "now" and allow all that you intend to be in your presence by being THAT! This sounds simple but it takes practice and yet we have all the time in the world to do practices for we have now, and now, and now, etc. There are many things to explore on planet earth and now is the time. Be in the moment as fully and as consciously as possible so that you may manifest your true divine potential. This varies for each individual but by connecting to the now and BE-coming YOU to the fullest (in the now) and as you become more and more aware, then more is available for you. Self-limiting beliefs are just that! Self-limiting; who wants to limit themselves? Well, many do unintentionally and many do with their mind-chatter of voice which is less than divine. Keep the thoughts higher and higher: raise them up as you raise up your awareness and your vibration will follow. You can do this; we all can. Notice the thoughts you have right now and if they are self-limiting then turn them around. You have the power over the mind so just switch it around! You can do this. Do you feel less than perfect? Well you are perfect so turn that around. The same goes with abundant and radiant and powerful and free. Switch it up and go for the highest of high for you deserve it: you are divine.

Yes you are.

Yes you are.

Blessed Be and God Bless YOU!

TODAY'S MESSAGE

Life is; you are; so it is. What will you make of it? This is
not a threat or a call to arms; this is a calling for awareness.
Awareness of the little things that make up your life; it
doesn't have to be "big" or "important" for it is all
important and yet simple and carefree because it JUST IS.
We are here to love one another: how are you doing with
that idea today? We are here to care for each other: how's
that working for you? There is much involved in the living,
in the energies, in the changing of the planet earth, in the
evolution of the human experience and most of this we
won't ever truly understand while we are here. BUT we can
live in love and light! We can be loving to our own soul's
growth and fond of our spirit! We can communicate and
relate to everything around our single-being-ness in order to
help others and self in order to learn. Life is a mystery and
you are amazing. Your life right here and right now is no
less than a miracle. Treat it as such as you interact with your
fellow man today and all that surrounds us here on planet
earth. Everything has consciousness; all just varies by
degrees. Increasing the awareness is a goal for all: rock, tree,
dog, squirrel, horse, child, man, woman and everything in
between.

LOVE AND LIGHT and go out there and

shine, shine, shine.

Shine brightly and LIVE freely.

God Bless.

TODAY'S MESSAGE

Step by step we move forward, stepping up into enlightenment. Sometimes it doesn't feel we are moving forward or moving up at all but that is just the process. Sometimes we may feel "stuck" in our stuff or as if we are "going backwards." It is all a process, so do not "beat yourself up" over it. Just start taking more steps, when you are ready. We know not our "true path" or how we are going to get to where we so desperately wish to go. Maybe now is not the time; maybe here is not the place; maybe you need to go through certain things to get to where and when you'll be more prepared to take the bigger leaps of faith. Have faith for the universe is working for you. The universe won't work for you when you feel great doubt and despair. CHINS UP, if you will. Don't give up on your dreams. Don't focus on the obstacles that may appear before you. Be in these moments, yes, and work through them, but keep your "eyes on the prize" as they say. This is easier said than done but the point here is to not give up hope. There are many twists and turns and bumps on everyone's path. Explore them and enjoy them and shine light on them so you release the fear and self-doubt around them. Focus on the greater outcome and the joy you have in the process. Staying in the process and not giving up hope is the key here. ALLOWING all that is, is the key here. Be brave and strong. Yesterday is history, as they say, and tomorrow is a mystery. Today is the main event; be ever present and stay focused and full of love. You can do it! There is greatness here; we believe in you. Have faith in self and the universe will act in kind. Love it all; embrace it all; find the joy and proceed ahead.

TODAY'S MESSAGE

Do what you can and enjoy what you are doing while you are doing it. There you go ~ enough said! Ha Ha! Of course, the above statement just may be the key to happy and healthy living. Whatever you are doing, if you are doing "this thing" while being full of "negativity" then it basically is not good for anyone. Lighten up! Enlighten up! Let's make everything we do more "high vibrational" by doing it with joy: eating, sleeping, working, playing, helping others and even being of service. Whatever we do with joy is infused with joy and those that receive, get more joy, and you, as the giver and doer, become more and more joy-filled. So let us find the joy in our hearts when it comes to our day to day. When you are doing something and it seems to be a chore, think of ways to "lighten" it up. If you find you cannot, possibly you may wish to leave those things behind. We are filled with love and energy when we are doing what we love ~ how simple is that? Let's find these things and do them more. Cut out the things that are wearing you down; do more things that build you up! If you are doing yoga and you don't have joy in your heart while doing it, then you are gaining more of those other feelings and emotions within the body. If you are eating something healthy and are angry about having to do so, then more anger fills the body. If you are watching television or are "online" and become full of rage, fear, and any "negative" feelings ~ can you see how you will be building those feelings up more and more in your body? Who needs that? Surround yourself with joy and light. It really can't be any easier than that. Want to become enlightened? This is a way to "lighten" up. ENJOY, IN JOY, AND HAVE A BLESSED DAY. LoveNLight!

TODAY'S MESSAGE

This space is yours; make it your own. This is not to say to take freedoms and free will away from others this is just to say that where you are and what you are doing can be more integrated as "your space" where you move your energies in and out and truly feel centered and grounded within. Create a circle in which you operate that comes along with you wherever you go. It can be a circle of energy around your car while driving or around your home or office when indoors. It can encompass the children when they are at school or at play. Use your energy core and heart energy to spread out into the world and ask for Arch Angel Michael to protect you and yours with that divine light. You can call on other Angels or Guides or Masters to help you do this as well. With help from the universe much can be created so do not forget to ask: one must ask to receive! Stay open and stay happy. Be loving and peace will enter your very soul.

Claim your energy; claim the energy around you and integrate. Love all and be blessed. You deserve it ~ it is your birthright to be happy. Let the fear go . . . move into your own protected energy space of clear and refined energy.

And have a blessed day.

For you:

LOVEANDLIGHT!

TODAY'S MESSAGE

All is well. All is well in the world. All is well within; when
you make it that way. We all live in the ups and downs of
life here on planet earth. How you show up for it all makes
a big difference. Going into things with fear and loathing
doesn't help much. Though fear can help you be on top of
your game for a work meeting or an interview but see how
peace can also do the same thing? The fear discussed here is
the fear that one often has that things are out of one's
control and that we most certainly want them in our control.
The outside world will never be under our control so why
waste that feeling? Instead replace that feeling of dread/fear
with that of love of the self and love of one's life and love
toward thy fellow man. We are here to be there for each
other; to love one another. You've heard this before but it is
worth repeating. When we show up with fear in our hearts
then we have less space for the love in our hearts and that is
where we can do the most good. And since most of us want
to be of service and "do good" then starting with the loving
heart-space is a wonderful thing. Start with it; end with it;
use it for the highest good for all mankind. You can do
great things that way! You can light up with world with just
the love coming from your heart. Your heart light connects
with others whose heart light is shining and then there is just
so much love . . . so much love for all.

For All Of Us.

God Bless.

TODAY'S MESSAGE

Feel your way. Go down deep and get into that intuitive feeling of what to do and when. Keep yourself clear though; when thoughts creep up that don't seem like "you" - make it stop and regroup. Many are having problems with these outside thoughts/influences/energies these days and it only takes a bit of conscientious effort to clear a path through the muck and mire so that you can rewire back to your soul-self; uninfluenced by the outside disturbances in the field, if you will. That is why many are not doing so well these days: they are full of fear and old programming and when the energy turns/fluctuates, then boom, crack, bang ~ they reactive in poor ways: ways they never ever thought or intended on. This is very sad and can be seen in much of the crime and depression and the general falling apart and those losing their mind/self. All of this is under your control: it just takes resolve and a conscious effort to LOOK, ACT, USE YOUR TOOLS FOR CLEARING, etc. etc. All is under your control. If you feel it isn't then the fear comes in and we give up more and more of our own thought/soul-mind abilities. So breathe; ground yourself. Let go of the fear mongering around you: STAY CLEAR OF IT! When it creeps in then notice it and clear yourself again and again. Let your thoughts be your own. Use your gut feelings and proceed forward. If your gut feelings/intuition feels off and does not follow your "ideal" (how you wish to live in each and every moment) then clear more (chakras, auras, mind energies) and try again. Keep trying. You'll get it! It just takes some practice and self-resolve. LOVE AND LIGHT and please be brave. **Focus on the beauty; always on the beauty.**

TODAY'S MESSAGE

Reach high; touch the stars. There is greatness in living here on planet earth at this time and most anything wonderful is possible. Sometimes it seems like it is not (possible) and that is when it won't be so change around that thought! Live in the gloriousness of life and find beauty in it ALL. That is another way to achieve your goals of life-happiness-everlasting. As we find glory in ALL things more gloriousness gravitates toward us making our world full of wondrous wonders. Life can be very full when we live in this way. The bird sings and we are filled with love and wonder. The leaf falls and we find the beauty. Babies cry and dogs bark and it is all songs to our ears. That is how the earth experience can work for us when our hearts are open. Think about a day when life seemed too much to bear; when that happens we often feel threatened or put out. When babies cry and dogs bark during these difficult times, you may have felt irritated. The wind blows and we become even more fearful and put out/put upon (basically feeling sorry for ourselves). But when we are open and in the flow not so much bothers us. This could be your reality for when we live in love then everything is a wonder.

Glorious earth; grateful living: happiness abound.

And the stars twinkle just for you.

LOVEANDLIGHT!

TODAY'S MESSAGE

Breathe.

Breathe again.

Breathe more deeply. Breathe in and out and focus on your heart-space. Rest; now breathe again and focus on your "high heart" and notice the ease there. Find your core strength in your gut and focus there as well. We are strong and courageous and all the rest seems much like the "divine play" where we will do our best to serve. At the same time, do know that much of this is just "the play" so breathe easy and play. We do our best and we should give ourselves a break. Look around and see the beauty ALL AROUND YOU. The people, the places; the animals and the wildlife and plants. Above us the heavenly stars and galaxies; the moon; the sun. We are blessed to have this beautiful planet in which to act out our "play." We have beautiful helpers to communicate with and interact with so that we may gain more knowledge and growth; so that we may learn our lessons: life lessons; eternal life lessons. How beautiful is that? And the sun shines and the winds blow and the rain falls and here we are . . . learning our lessons. It is a gift and the sooner we embrace it (lovingly and willingly) the sooner we will ascend in our learning, our gifts, our lessons, as well as our Vibration. To life! To light! To the highest of Vibration! And we continue on . . . breathing deeply and breathing from the heart.

LOVEANDLIGHT!

TODAY'S MESSAGE

Everything is important.

Despite what your "plans" are for today, do find importance
in each interaction. Even with strangers, even with
"chores;" do take this day for a time of important
interactions with everyone and every living thing.
Everything is alive, as many say; they all have energies: even
the rocks, the trees; the wind. All is alive so treat it as such.
This can be made seen in the interactions. As you work with
certain elements you will hear and feel a response. Then
more respect comes to these things and your interactions
with such and we ALL become more of a whole-life-form
working for the benefit of the good/the god: the whole. If
you can be kind to a rock and tree and animal then of course
you can find the time to be kind to other human beings:
those of your own "kind." Those that may make difficulties
for you and/or those you find too different from yourself
that you don't want to "go there" - work with them as well.
Always with the high vibration that is you. That lifts us all
up. Don't dim our light: let it shine upon all that is living so
that it may benefit. You are love and light. Work with all the
important interactions today and make a brighter and lighter
world. It is your world so let it shine and glow with your
high vibrational energy and you will "be there," living in this
new paradigm of love and light; of joy and giving.

Blessings to you on this fine day!

TODAY'S MESSAGE

Each day is precious: do take the "intention" of making every day precious, including this glorious day. Each of us experiences their own reality so create your experience to align with that which is perfect and good. Of course things happen that seem less than perfect but do allow, lovingly and willingly, ALL that comes into your experience. It is as simple (and as complex) as that. Be who you are and the universe will sing your praises: just for being who you are: truly in mind/body/spirit/soul energy. When we work "against" ourselves, we limit ourselves and the world needs the true you. Your true authentic self is "where it's at" so just be there, just be yourself and enjoy the experience. Oftentimes we wear masks to cover our true selves for we feel others will not accept us as we are. You are you so you might as well act like it ~ only then can you find your "soul purpose" ~ that what you are supposed to be doing here on planet earth. Wearing a mask is probably not your soul purpose. Acting and being who you are will better align you to that. See? As you are, so you will be, and from there you will glean a better understanding of self. Things change and people change. Find who you are: find that core of you. The world is waiting and the universe has put you here for a reason.

Be it.

Claim it!

For all is perfect; as are you. You are perfect!

TODAY'S MESSAGE

Take time to settle in.

Take time to settle into the new energies of the planet and the new energies within. Take time to process the things you feel: even the hurts and the pain. Allow things to flow as freely as possible. Fighting it only prolongs the process. Let things flow within and through you. Become an "empty vessel." Then the light fills you up, see? Many do not like the idea of becoming an empty vessel for they feel they would "lose themselves." The fact of the matter is that the opposite can be said to be true. As you free yourself of that which you hold onto: the victim role, the titles, the "masks" and the placement of such in society, etc., then you find your true essence. It is that which has always been you ~ from time immemorial. It is your free and bare soul light shining through. Allow today. Make room for the light. Release the rest for it no longer serves you in this higher energy of consciousness. Relax and take heed for all is well in the world and you are gorgeous.

Take time to process that - You Are Gorgeous!

LOVE AND LIGHT TODAY AND EVERY DAY.

God Bless.

TODAY'S MESSAGE

What can you do to help the world? That is a good question or idea to live by. Many times we focus on other things as being the "most important thing" such as money and relationships and there are just a variety of different things humans focus on. But the idea/l of being helpful is a great ideal to live by. This is not the kind of help that may make you sweat and toil but if that is gratifying for you to work in that realm then the universe approves. Sometimes we can be helpful by the wave of the hand or a smiling attitude. Other times it may be lifting someone up who has stumbled and just the old adage of "giving someone a leg up;" giving someone a hand: helping thy brother. This way of life creates joy in the actions and joy in the being. It helps the giver as much (or more) than those who receive. It provides a sense of purpose and even a sense of peace. Helping others can even become addictive! Try it and you will feel such great joy and purpose that you will want to continue. Also, helping others makes the world go round: there is a feeding of the energy and then an increase in the energy (due to joy and communion) and then more energy for others and self and on and on and on. There is greatness in being a giver. Thank you all who work in this light for there are many. When you are feeling down and forlorn and forgotten, it may just be that you stopped helping others. Try it and see if that brings you back around to your loving joyous self.

LOVEANDLIGHT today and all days.

TODAY'S MESSAGE

Love and light to you today and all days. It is good to laugh it off: whatever your day has been like and however you find yourself, do find laughter and joy as well. There is much we can do here on planet earth and we can find love and laughter along the way: in all things; in all things. There is greatness here and there is the duality and we often find ourselves saying "this day sucks" or "this day is wonderful" where instead we can just BE in the day and say, "here I am!" That is a good day when we are present and just lovingly and willingly BE-ing with all things. Of course people are people and they act certain ways and that is fine too - but how do YOU want to be? More joyous? More loving? Find the gratitude for the living experience and this all comes together nicely. We live, we laugh, we cry, we mourn, we lose, we win and we are still "in it" and learning; always learning. We might as well be joyous for ALL the days. Not just the holidays or weekends but all that is. You are here right now: this is your life right now. Love, light, laughter, joy: find it ~ it is your birthright; it is natural and it is yours. Claim it and be glad in it. That is all. That is all we need to do. Just live. Stop the worry; lose the fear; welcome the joy.

Amen.

Love and light to you on this fine day.

LOVEANDLIGHT!

TODAY'S MESSAGE

Wherever you are; so you BE. BE in where you are and really revel in it. BE ever present and BE full of gratitude wherever you find yourself. Sometimes we are sick and at other times feeling on top of the world. We need not be the same (steady current) all the time. However, we can just "BE" in it (wherever that may be) and get something out of the experience. Simply by recognizing yourself and your place within the universe and those around you, we gain. Having more awareness is always a good thing for then we speak more from a place of truth as we recognize ourselves and whence we came. Life isn't a place to always know everything, however, just the idea that you are "there" within the life and that you are aware of the living is the greatest part: even if you are lost or afraid or unsure. Just be in it. Even being lost can provide clarity! We are so lucky to be here on planet earth right now. We can do many things here and the "atmosphere" is changing where more and more can become manifest. This is a joyous time and a time to stay connected. There is no reason to disengage any longer. We are here; we are living in fullness and bliss. We are awake and there is no need to close our eyes for we are here and here is a perfect place to be.

Realize, relax and enjoy.

Just BE.

TODAY'S MESSAGE

We are about to embark on the journey of a lifetime; are you ready? Of course your journey, your life, is a journey of a lifetime and every second of every day you are in it. Are you in it fully and with great reverence, acceptance and joy? That would be a good way to be. Even though we are each embarking on our own journey, the planet is also embarking on a journey and you are here to witness. Can you feel the change in the weather, a change in the air, a change in the leaving of the old ways and the starting of the new? It is much like your life in that much is changing but we are focused on the here and now and we don't see the change so much but often we can feel it and that is the way with the earth changes. Some are slower to accumulate and others strike fast and furious and are then gone like the wind. All is well and good in this regard. Too much change all at once is sometimes too difficult to comprehend so do give yourself time to process your own changes and growth and revelations: your new understandings. All is well in this regard and all is well in the world. Note the changes and process; breathe and move forward. Rest when you need to and stay healthy in the body/mind/spirit. Do what it takes to keep yourself happy and focused and feeling one with the world. We ARE one so it is great when you can feel it and use the oneness love energy to feed your soul. Love and light and take it easy on yourself. Take time for your processing and breathe. Stay strong in your light for you are so worthy and so needed. God Bless: every one of us.

TODAY'S MESSAGE

There are great things happening here on planet earth and
great things happening within you: as above so below as
within so without (the outside occurrences). All is in perfect
order. If your life seems not in perfect order then so be it;
that is life. But the order within self should be strong. The
resolve and the ideal and the drive can be put in order and
maximized at this time. Believe in that strength within and
do not waiver. Of course when we are dealing with others
we leave much wiggle room and compassion. When
working with self we can do so too (flowing with the
rhythms of the earth and the moon and the
body/mind/spirit system). This is all well and good. The
idea here is to get your house in order (mind/spirit) so that
you stay strong. When there is the wavering, then listen.
What is the problem; how can I resolve it; does it come from
my past (most probably); am I missing something. Find the
imbalance and work with it to create peace around that
"issue." We are all doing quite fine here on planet earth.
Find the goodness within self and make right within so you
can better deal without (the outside factors and people).

See?

LOVEANDLIGHT TODAY

AND ALL DAYS.

BLESSINGS; BLESSINGS; BLESSINGS.

TODAY'S MESSAGE

Breathe deep; get grounded. Be present; get happy. So many things we can think about in our day. How are your thoughts? If they seem scattered, then any of the above will help. As we breathe deep we connect with our inner spirit and we come into our bodies. This is important for being "grounded" is so important right now. If we are flying here and there with our thoughts and we neglect the body, it will remind us through pain and illness. If we forget to rest the body and provide it with good sustenance, the same occurs. Pain and illness are simply the body speaking to you about what it needs; what it lacks; what you've forgotten. This is fine for when pain and illness come we can take a deep breath and look at what is wrong with the body. Or we can practice this all the time: staying grounded and staying connected to the body, so that it need not speak back with such issues, see? Of course if you are sick or in pain now you can ask the body what you can do to feel better. You can work though what is happening on the physical that most likely is even related to your mental and spiritual you as well. There are many ways to communicate and work with the body temple. The best thing you can do is to love yourself and honor the body for all it does for you. It will respond in kind. Loving thoughts, loving words, food and drink provided with love will get you a long way.

LOVE THYSELF!

HONOR THY BODY!

TODAY'S MESSAGE

What would it take for you to live by love; the law of one; the great conception? It wouldn't take much to make love your ideal: the way you wish to live your life and how you conduct yourself in all things. Of course the practice is difficult at times but it is a wonderful "ideal" and good starting point. Edgar Cayce used to speak of having an ideal for your life: a fallback plan; a way in which you conduct yourself and/or your service to mankind. An ideal can be peace or integrity or a variety of things. Anything positive would make a beautiful starting point for your interactions and your conduct. Let love be our ideal for today. Let us live in love. Let us love our lives and our "vessels" (ourselves) and let our interactions be filled with love. Let our whole being be permeated with the loving light of source/god and let us walk THAT path. It won't be easy but it may be easier (and more rewarding) than you might think. Love is the answer; love is the ideal "ideal." Love is perfect as are you. Blessings to you on this fine day. God Bless and get out there and put love into the mix.

LOVE AND LIGHT TODAY

AND

ALL DAYS

FOR ALL MEN

IN ALL WAYS.

TODAY'S MESSAGE

We are one with the earth and all her inhabitants. Many turn away from this idea but the fact remains: we are one. This is how things were set up here on planet earth as well as other star systems. It just is this thing; this oneness. The only problem with this fact is that many do not believe it AND/OR they do not live like it is the truth. It would be wonderful if more and more people saw what we really are; that more and more people awaken to the truth: the laws of the universe; the law of one. Much in our society says me, me, me and much of our mind/thoughts are very egocentric or self-motivated and driven. This is the paradox; almost the idea that we are already set up for failure to understand this law of one. Or it can be seen as a wonderful challenge. Many have looked beyond the idea of duality and this is just another lesson ~ to look beyond the idea of INDIVIDUALITY and the ego and start understanding and even embracing the law of one. We come from source and from there we shall return. There will be no individuality when we are in the mix of the loving light of oneness on the "other side." Let us find some of that, just a bit of that feeling, while here on earth. Look at the earth mother ~ she is crying for you to see her as part of you. Look at the animals and plants. Look at your brothers and sisters. They've all been hurt by the separation. Unite in the light. It is where we need to be. It is our only hope. Division is death and unity is life.

To life!

TODAY'S MESSAGE

Stay focused. Stay focused on the light in your heart and the love in your soul-being. Be full of joy today; there is much to be joyous about. We get scattered and look in all directions when we can actually function better grounded, through our heart and core, and with love all around our being/aura/energy fields. This is something we can work on today. When the cluttered thoughts creep in we can stop and breathe and find our joy; find out love-space and go there. Pull in the energy of the heavens/cosmos just by imagining that you are like a tree. Your branches are reaching up to the universe and sun and pulling that energy down within your energy body. Then imagine that your roots are growing deep deep into mother earth and you feel your connection there. Imagine that earth loving mother energy coming up through your core and heart and into all cells of your body. Both the above and below energy connects through your heart and core. You can even imagine that the energy from above and the energy from below begin to spiral like a DNA double helix running up and down your body. Then go back to your tree image and imagine all your leaves are colorful and full of bright and strong love and light and they touch those in need. This energy is forever present and will nourish you and all others in your reach. All is perfect.

We move forward in love and light.

No fear.

TODAY'S MESSAGE

Let the light and love of the infinite oneness fill your mind/body/spirit and rejuvenate your soul-essence. There is greatness in the light. There is oneness in the love. Can you get to that love space that is compassion for ALL THINGS (not just for some)? Love for all the situations in your life. Love for your fellow man. Love for yourself? This is a place you should be heading. This is a place where you can live in peace regardless of what is happening around you. There is much in the way of fear-tactics at play here on planet earth at this time. Watch your thoughts for when you become part of the fear, you lose judgment and then the "picking sides" and then the condemning and then hate happens within your being. You ask to live in love and light so this is one way to move toward it ~ every time you move AWAY from fear is a move toward the light. As the little song goes, "let it go; let it go." Let go of the fear for we are ONE and we need to cultivate that oneness love within our hearts so we can truly live it; be it. Feel it and live it and expand on that so your loving essence extends out into the world. It is needed, my friends, it is needed. Don't allow fear to create darkness in your soul. Lift up from the lower vibratory masses and see the light above: it is there and it is beautiful; as are you.

Keep strong.

It is important,

for the WHOLE.

TODAY'S MESSAGE

Find your core; find your balance. There is much in the way of topsy-turvy energy these days: sometimes we feel on top of the world and sometimes we feel we are spinning out of control. This is fine when we can navigate from a strong core of being. We are energy/spiritual beings living in a physical body. We can use our mind/energy and our spiritual side to strengthen the physical so there is less and less side-effects of change. It is important right now to be as clear as possible, for our chakras to be clear and aligned, and for our bodies to be balanced. It is also important to clear up our residual fears, memories and issues that are holding us back. These issues have an energetic hold so that we are actually "still back there" in those "negative circumstances." That is why to move forward in love and light we ask these old issues be cleared. There are so many holistic modalities to clear us up: check them out and find what resonates with you. And of course this doesn't all happen in one session or as quickly and as easily as one might hope but it does happen and for each and everything you can let go of from the past, the better for you to grow in the light. For each time you balance and heal yourself the better you will feel and the clearer you will think and act (and the less you will "re"act due to old programming (memories/fears/issues). It is as simple and as awesomely complex and wonderful as that. Get healed. There are many ways to do this. Start working on yourself is important and if you started before and then felt you couldn't go any further then by all means try again. This work has a cumulative effect: it is all good. Now is the time and your body/vessel is the place. Love it. Love it. Love it ALL for the whole of life we live is just glorious. Be happy and move forward. Let the burdens of the past go.

TODAY'S MESSAGE

Everything is perfect today. Do you not feel this is the case? In your life, right here and now, during this reading time, do you not have all you need? Things often seem too big to handle. The world's problems and even individual problems seem too great to change/resolve/move on from and/or be happy despite it all. But right here and right now you are okay, right? You are breathing and reading and you are relatively relaxed. That is how it can always be in life as we focus on the "now." Stay loving and strong and yet relaxed in each and every second of the now. Of course things need to be done quickly at times and we can speed up our now (or slow it down accordingly) but the idea here is to stay focused on this: that right here and right now you are okay; you have all you need. The world is changing and you are changing and the people around you are changing but again, guess what, it is all okay. Many things can be changed and will be changed (or there will be an allowance and change will happen, especially when it comes to earth changes). Just focus on the now and the breath and the beautiful life that is given you. Be grateful and take heart: all is perfect as are you. Breathe and find your core.

Breathe and relax and take it one step at a time;

one breath at a time.

LOVEANDLIGHT!

TODAY'S MESSAGE

Use your intuition: feel your way. The times are changing.
There is much energy behind living in the flow and going
where and how and when by using our INTUITION. You
know that feeling you get where you are sure about things
because it just feels right? This makes life more flowing
when we act with our intuition-feelings behind us and "in
our corner." When you feel hesitant then check-in and ask
your "inner voice" and/or knowing and LISTEN. Another
idea that may seem opposite of this is working THROUGH
issues that don't seem so pleasant when you "check in."
Your intuition-feelings may not be talking and/or seems
"negative." We can work through these situations as well by
being focused with intention. Instead of avoiding the issue,
even though it feels heavy, we can intend for things to
manifest a certain way and ask for the highest and best good
of all as you proceed ahead. This is the idea that we need
not always wait for our intuition to say GO. If there are
things you feel you need to do (intuition is telling you this
anyway) and yet it doesn't "feel good" in your body ~ you
can still work through it and allow for the grace to flow
through it all as well. There are many ways one can function
in this world and those are just a few. Being conscious is the
key. Affirmations and intentions and working with your
intuitive side and inner voice: these are all very conscious
ways of living. When we live consciously we have less
"backlash" for we are more aligned AND less reactive and
more pro-active which is a good way to be. Just less
"consequences" that way. And when the consequences do
arise? Then we accept them lovingly and willingly and
proceed again openly for the highest and best good. Again,
this is just one way to live, it is totally up to you.

TODAY'S MESSAGE

We are all one.

We are part and parcel of the great I AM.

How great are you feeling today? You should be feeling great and powerful for the great I AM is great and powerful. You should feel that all your dreams may become manifest for the I AM presence can manifest anything. We have all we need. This is something one should affirm each and every day: "I have all I need; I am provided for; I am, as I am; I am part and parcel of the One Source - the great I AM." This affirmation will create a sense of wonder for each and every one of us who utters the sounds. OMMM is another sound one can repeat and Shalom is another. Shanti Shanti Shanti and Peace provides peace within. That is a good one to mantra as well. Do use these tools. Thoughts are powerful and words are more powerful still. Our feelings of lack give us nothing but fear and more lack coming to us (or more examples to make us think we are in lack). So let us turn that around and feel great and powerful for you come from the One Source and from there you shall return. Have a blessed day and stay strong in the light. When you feel your light is fading then use the tools, use the mantras and affirmations to raise-up your vibration so you can receive. Blessings Love and Light to ALL MEN; today and every day.

Amen.

PEACE. SHANTI.

TODAY'S MESSAGE

Life is; you ARE; and we are all together! See? We are all together on this planet; on this journey called life. Each and every one of us has that in common ~ we are one and each of us are brothers and sisters on earth. Many of us choose who is important and who is special and who is less than and who is the enemy. And yet we are all here right now and have so much in common. We wish our children to be happy; we wish for a safe planet. It is just that different groups go about this idea differently. Each of us decides what we feel is best and that is often not taking in "the group" in their considerations for we often forget that we are ONE. Yes, there are wars, and yes, there are those suffering. But yet, there is love here and yes, we are all brothers and sisters. Most animals and other wildlife use group life-giving forces but humans often times see themselves as more individuals/more independent. In olden times there was more of a group life-giving idea but not so much any longer. What can you do today to help ALL of mankind? One may think of many ideas to do this and feel "their way" is the way to help. This is fine but what I am asking is for you to look in your heart and see your humanity as a group and those you may feel are your enemy as actually your brothers and sisters. In sum, find peace within your own heart and mind. When we vow to be a part of humanity through love, we can succeed. When we feel it is best to "wipe out" others, we do not succeed. Not as the group called humanity. Let us lift up EVERYONE! Find that in your heart is all we ask. LOVEANDLIGHT and have a blessed day.

TODAY'S MESSAGE

Everything happens in its own time. This has been said before but of course, like many concepts, is worth repeating. We have our own agenda and the universe works as the universe works ~ sometimes NOT on our agenda. Having our own agenda often mixes us up. It is always nice to concede with allowing the universe and the higher powers to guide us instead. Asking for the highest and best good of all involved and according to universal divine timing is perfect.

Much can happen under those pretexts. Asking for something you desperately want to happen "right now" is not as fruitful for several reasons. One would be that you are "desperate" for it. When we are desperate we are not in alignment for we have lost our faith. Also, wanting things to happen NOW is not in alignment either for there are so many considerations at play. The universe can't bend to your every whim (lol) nor may it be in your best interest to get what you so desperately want at that exact time. This is where the idea of "flow" comes into the equation. This is where the idea of being in service to the higher source/greater good comes into play as well. For when we align to that "greater purpose" we won't be so desperate and we can also be more patient, and loving, at the same time so that more perfect things come into our experience. Let the universe provide for you. Allow it to happen when the timing is right. Allow your own fears and desperation around what you want to fade so that you can feel happy and at peace where you are right now. Get aligned and be happy with the timing of the universe. Be happy and more and more will come into your experience that creates happiness and joy for you.

TODAY'S MESSAGE

Today is beautiful, as are you.

There is much beauty in the world: it is wonderful to focus on that. There are the greatest of things here on planet earth and much is possible; with love and focus and good intentions we can manifest anything! Sometimes people get frustrated for they try and try to manifest things in their life and they fall short. Having an acceptance of all that is and the higher universe being on your side is a good way to look at those times when we feel we have fallen short on manifesting our dreams. Our dreams are still our dreams and there is much time to allow things to fall into place. You are not out of time! Align yourself to the highest of source and stand in that light. Be a "servant" of good and love and at the same time ask for what you wish for. This universe is abundant beyond our wildest dreams. Don't let the past get you down for those times you've tried and "not succeeded." You are great as is the infinite powers of the universe. Align yourself there and stay focused on your dreams.

It is wonderful to focus on a life full of love and wonder.

Those dreams will surely become manifest.

LOVEANDLIGHT

TODAY'S MESSAGE

We can learn and grow from many kinds of situations. It doesn't always have to be painful and it doesn't necessarily need to be through teaching situations. Most soul growth learning happens with simple living. So if you are living and relatively open to change then you are learning. It is as easy at that! Just show up and be open to life. There is much greatness to living on planet earth at this time and we often get bogged down and forget to look at the blessings in the lessons. We also forget to acknowledge all the blessings.

The sunshine and a safe home are wonderful blessings. Food to eat and water to drink; friends and family: all great blessings. Have you been thankful lately? Sometimes we forget but when we take the time to be appreciative for all we have and all there is it makes life seem even more magical. There are many who are suffering and even those who have their needs met in the staples of life (food, drink, safe housing) they suffer too. It is a hierarchy of things one can suffer over, though I say to you, just be open and be happy for the blessings that come your way. Help others to ease their burdens (which will feed your soul) and again be open for the learning that comes with living. These simple tools can create a life of plenty. Do know that it takes your "investment," however, it takes your consciousness.

All is perfect, as are you.

BLESSINGS LOVEANDLIGHT TODAY AND ALL DAYS.

FOREVERMORE.

TODAY'S MESSAGE

You are the light of the world. We are the light of the world. Each and every one of us helps join together to bring the light to planet earth. Many feel the sunlight is giving light and it most certainly is. Many feel the love of the earth radiating through their bodies as well. This is a beautiful thing: Father Sky and Mother Earth working together to heal us and make us grow. At the same time, let us think of gathering these energies and having them meet at our heart-space. Allow the love and light of the heavens and the earth feed our souls. There is much "there for us" that we forget about. There is a great plan that we do not know about ~ that is fine. All is fine. All is good. You can find the love and light of the divine AROUND YOU and WITHIN YOU. You can allow this light to shine out into the world to heal others as it is healing you. No one can take your light away and as you give, so you receive more from source/s. Rest when you need to but at the same time, tap into the cosmic energies and earth energies and nurture yourself and others. All is perfect; as are you. Do find the beauty in all things. Especially find beauty in your own heart: it is there, do not deny it. The light and love of your heart is "dying" to explode out to help others. Tap it; feed it; shine it out to all mankind. We need it and when you let your light shine, your heart sings with joy (as does the heavens and the earth).

BLESSINGS BLESSINGS LOVEANDLIGHT.

TO ALL.

ALL.

TODAY'S MESSAGE

Do take time to open up to the world today. It is not such a bad place despite what the news and media may have you believe. There is great joy here; there is much to learn here as well. This is a nice way to live in the world: open for the experiences. This has been said before. Let's "up this" a bit more, and go from not just being open to our experiences, but to do so LOVINGLY and WILLINGLY - enduring all things. This idea is another from Dr. John Whitman Ray who was mentioned in yesterday's channeling. It actually doesn't matter who said what when ~ these are simply tools and/or different ways of working with your life experiences ~ allowing you to enjoy your life more and more each day. You could try one tool on one day and another on another day but the idea here is to give some of these "ideas" a try and see what works for you. What works for you today may be different than what will work for you tomorrow AND the best thing about this is that there is an accumulative effect of all the work you do on yourself. We are building up to be better human beings. Just trying is a very brave thing to do.

So for today our "challenge" is to endure (or maybe ENJOY) all things lovingly and willingly.

All experiences are lessons:

work with them by using your tools.

LOVE AND LIGHT TO ALL MEN:

ALL OF US;

no exceptions.

TODAY'S MESSAGE

Life is beautiful just the way it is. Do enjoy (in-joy) each and every moment you have here on planet earth. Sometimes life, and the world, seems troubling and/or confusing. It may seem sad or scary. Life and the world can seem any aspect of emotion/feeling . . . how do you want to see the world today? Do find yourself in a place of peace/no fear. Do work on that today. There are great changes happening here on planet earth and you are HERE to experience it. So experience it. Don't run away from it. Don't hide from it. Don't fear it: be joyful IN IT. Life is beautiful when we experience things to the fullest expression. Sometimes we forget the basis of love and light in our body/mind/spirit and then living "full-on" can seem harsh. That is when we need to get back to the garden, as they say: back to the loving light of the creator. Place that love and light in your heart and it will clear the mind. Stay as connected as humanly possible and be glad in it. Love is here for you. Light is here for you. We are here for you. Blessings love and light to all of humanity: every single solitary person. And of course blessings to all the other glorious living creatures on earth today.

LOVE AND LIGHT

AND

KEEP THE FAITH!

TODAY'S MESSAGE

Where is your focus today? That is your world; your experience. Whatever you focus on is basically that. We can focus on all kinds of things: love and laughter, family and friends, or those things considered "worse" or "more difficult" can also be focused on and therefore becomes your experience. Life is working like that more and more these days ~ where we focus becomes our reality. So, as been said before, watch what you are focusing ON! We can focus on a "theme" about our lives by using what Edgar Cayce once talked about: "our ideal." This can be the theme for how we want to live in the world (through love, with integrity, focusing on source, etc. etc.). Your ideal is from you, from your heart and it is a good guideline to work within. You will notice when you are working outside of this ideal for you will feel "not so pleasant." One can also create affirmations for their day and that is another nice way to set up your experiences. They can be personal as well: "I am strong and beautiful," or "I am healthy, wealthy, and wise." The thing about affirmations is that they really work best when you actually FEEL them to be true so it may take many repeats of the affirmation for the feelings/beliefs to sink in. So that is another good way to create your reality.

One last way to create your beautiful world is simply working with the feelings; those feelings deep down in your body. When you FEEL loved and cared for, then more and more of THAT will come into your experience. Have a lovely day and God Bless (everyone: every single one of us now and forever).

TODAY'S MESSAGE

There is a time and a purpose for all things, as they say, and of course this is worth repeating. This is something to contemplate today as the day unfolds. Having an allowance of all things that come into your experience and making the most of them is a beautiful way to live. Sometimes we forget and we scream "why, why, why???" But we know not all there is to know in this reality and we really just don't know everything; we really don't. That is another good thought for today: we just don't know everything and how and why things play out like they do BUT we can be appreciative of "it all," nonetheless. There is much to do here on planet earth and there are great things happening. There is the idea of "trust" that is so important. And with trust we gain faith. And with faith we gain contentment/joy/peace. It is all a process and being aware of our process is another good thing to look at today. Be open in the experience and be loving in the exchange. That is all we can do and it is perfect. Everything is perfect as are you. Keep trying! Keep looking up! Blessings to ALL MEN: ALL MEN WITH NO EXCEPTIONS.

Only then will gain peace on this planet and finding peace in

YOU is the first step.

LOVEANDLIGHT TODAY AND ALL DAYS.

Blessings ~

TODAY'S MESSAGE

Make the most of your day, your hours, your minutes and seconds: all the special moments of your life. Do savor those. We are here for a reason ~ to experience ~ so let's take those experiences and really get into them. Again, the idea of being very conscious in all we do. There is more to life when we live in this way: everything becomes a big deal and everything should be a big deal for every second is precious. There are great things here on earth and our connections with others should be considered paramount. If you are feeling isolated, then make a vow to "get out there more" and mix and mingle. Shake it up and meet others of your kind and others who may be different. Notice your actions and take action to be the best you can be in every circumstance. At times you may fall short of being kind and generous and loving but the more we try, the better we will gain over the old ways; those times when we were led by temptation and lower energy vibrations: programming. Living fully will be a thrill ride enough; there will be no need for "altered states" for this state, the state of higher consciousness, is the highest and the deepest and the most expansive of experiences. Be THAT and be happy and be full of life. This is your birthright, as they say, this is living.

GOD BLESS ALL MEN.

ALL MEN: EVERY SINGLE ONE OF US;

NO EXCEPTIONS.

TODAY'S MESSAGE

Let us stay strong in our core; our heart beat and our purpose. If that seems too great a challenge then breathe, breathe, breathe. Now, again, think back to the core, the heart beat, your purpose. Let us keep working toward that with every breath. This can be done by concentrating on the beating of your heart or imagine "breathing in and out of your heart-space." That gets you more heart-centered. Our core can be strengthened with breathing in and out of that area and/or by imagining energy from mother earth coming into the body and finding its way there. We can also imagine the energy of the cosmos coming down and meeting in the lower chakras as well. Create an infinity symbol swirl of energy and imagine it strengthening with limitless energy. There you go: some heart centered focus and core strength for you. And then living from the soul purpose, that is easy to do as well when concentration is focused there. What makes you happy? What do you feel you just "must do" regardless of money or fame? Well, that is your soul's purpose and guess what? When you work toward that, you are strengthening you core and living from your heart space anyway. How beautiful is that? Do know that staying strong is important these days as there are great energies aflutter. Your strength is vital for your soul's growth so do be vigilant in your practice and that can be as simple as taking your concentration there: to the heart, your core and your soul's purpose. You are doing a great job! Keep strong and keep up the good (light) work. Blessings love and light to ALL MEN. ALL. ALL OF US; NO EXCEPTIONS. **AMEN.**

TODAY'S MESSAGE

Take each moment for what it is. USE it for your own growth and evolution. BE in it in the fullest expression of self; more fully "in the scene." Let us take some time today to amp up our progression by being fully present in each and every moment. If you are in a rest mode, then be fully present there. If you are with family, then be fully present there. If you are working, then be fully present! What can you learn? Who can you be? How beautiful can you make this moment? Living in this way is so humbling at times and so energizing at other times. BE-ing gives us great strength as we work on action versus RE-action. Reacting is the old way we did things; that which is in our patterning and codes. Action is living from a higher law and a more conscious law.

That doesn't mean we always get it right or have the best behavior but the more consciously aware we are, the more consciously aware we shall act, and this does something for our souls. It aligns us; it shows us our old codes; it moves us away from "outside" and/or "old programming" It pulls us out of the darkness and into the light: into awareness. Let us take the masks off and be REAL today.

Let us do our best and shine brightly.

We can use a bit more brightness here on planet earth ~

TODAY'S MESSAGE

All you need is love, so they say. Of course we need food and water and good air but let us look at the idea of "all you need is love." This is not to say you need someone loving on you or even you loving on someone else. This is to say that there is a better way of working here on planet earth and that is in and through LOVE. It is like "being in love" but you are just in love with everything. It is like using love as your guide and your final answer. It is like painting everything you do with love. You may say that this is difficult to do for there is so much to be upset and angry about these days and that these "other" feelings often dominate your life and situations. This is probably true and living from love may not seem like the easiest thing to do but it can be quite rewarding when we decide to place ourselves under its spell. A way to do this is by noticing our actions/reactions/feelings to different situations and then asking "what would love do?" This does not need to take a long time and much contemplation need not go into it for you can actually "feel" it very quickly. Does this feel like love? No. Then ask: what would love do? Now that isn't so hard to do, is it? If you are feeling depleted and angry these days do try this simple task. You and those around you will surely notice a difference. And if not, no worries, for you would be living under the higher law and that is an admirable thing to do.

Even in the trying; even in the prayer.

Blessings to you on this fine day.

TODAY'S MESSAGE

One breath at a time and one step at a time ~ this has been said quite often these days but it is important right now to not get "too overwhelmed." There is much happening on and around planet earth right now and the most important thing you can do is keep yourself on the straight and narrow path of love and light. This takes focus and strength and breath and the greatest of courage. Feel your determination for the "right way" and stick with it one action at a time. Breathe and rest and take your time in making decisions and acting on them. Let go of the worry and work with what you've got right now. There is always time for more; just know there is much happening right now and keeping our "head straight" is very important. This idea can be also applied by changing your focus and living within the "heart space." That, in and of itself, creates the clearer head for you are "letting that go" and working from the heart instead. There is much to do on planet earth and much time to do it so for today, deep breathing, concentration and living from the heart.

Blessings to you and all men; today and every day.

God Bless.

TODAY'S MESSAGE

Let us stop and breathe. Let us take a "little breather" here. Oftentimes we get so worked up on what we are supposed to be doing we forget to be. We even forget the doing for we are focused too far ahead; too far afield. Being in the "now" is often the message for the day and today it is especially important. Many of us are wondering what will happen next and how we are going to "get there." Let us worry (not worrying; just focus) on NOW instead. Not the future, not the past, but what we are doing in the right here and right now is where to place the focus. Again, this has been said before but how to do this, you may ask: what is the best way? There is never a "best way" that works "across the board" for everyone . . . there are different ways for different people but there are a few constants that should be considered: the breath, the connection, and meditation are KEY! When have you meditated last? Many say, "I'm in a constant state of meditation." Really? Let's be truthful with self. If there is the banter in the mind then you are not in constant meditation. TAKE THE TIME to do the work! Use the tools for self-reflection, self- empowerment, and clearing/understanding. That which you seek is right there in the breath, in the connection, and in the meditative properties. There are no short-cuts. We must do the work and remain vigilant in our focus. At the same time let us be free floating and joyous too. Can we do both?

Of course we can. Find the balance.

LOVE AND LIGHT and have a beautiful day.

TODAY'S MESSAGE

Take each moment and savor it. Be the best you can be
during that moment while finding strength and courage in
each second you are alive. Pull in more and more LIFE and
joy into your being. Of course we need to rest at times too
so do know there are the cycles . . . just as the moon cycles
the tides and winds, so to do outer affects your
body/mind/spirit, so rest when you need to. Regardless, the
idea here is to savor life. Even if it is resting time you can
savor that too! Drink it in. Appreciate each moment
without "waiting" for that time where everything will be
perfect. Right now is perfect; work with now and enjoy it.
Life is beautiful when we can do this. And you will gain
more and more power and happiness as you do. Life is for
the living so LIVE IT! Be not afraid. When you feel the
fear, take a look at it and notice what oftentimes it really is:
False Evidence Appearing Real (f.e.a.r.). So just go for it!
Look fear in the eyes (in your own eyes) and refuse to be
limited.

Break the patterns; break the chains.

Live free and fully present.

LOVE AND LIGHT!

TODAY'S MESSAGE

Take it easy! Take it easy on yourself and your "process."
We spend much time fighting an internal fight that is most
times not "called for." Do give yourself credit! You are
doing the best you can with what you have right here and
now. The sins of the past are in the past and maybe they
weren't so bad after all. We know not why things happen so
allow that that WAS the way ("it was") and work on the way
it IS. HERE is where it's at! Of course we can look at our
past to clean and clear things up. Even when we performed
"okay" in certain situations we can take a good look back
and evaluate the "programs" and patterns in which we
typically live. Let us start breaking down those patterns so
we can live more freely and more consciously. What was
done in the past was most likely "reactionary" and now we
can work the other way: standing in our power and light,
being conscious and pure and clean of the past and focused
on the now. Let's do that and let's be easy on our hearts and
souls; our mind and body. Let us actually go a bit further
and HONOR ourselves and our process. Let us raise that
up a notch and become even JOYOUS in all things. Now
that's the way to live! Can you do that? You can; you really
can. Raise it up! Raise it up! Raise it up! Enjoy your day, in
joy, and IN HONOR of self and all that is. We are here
right now: let's make the best of it. Like REALLY best ~
like joy and love and light abound kind of best.

This is your birthright.

Step up into the joy; your life and God Bless.

TODAY'S MESSAGE

Be happy! Why not ~ might as well. Yes, things seem to "falling apart" around the world these days but your happiness is quite important in the scheme of things. That may seem counter-intuitive but it is true. The more joy in this world the more joy in this world; as simple as that. This idea is simple and yet many may say, "how can I smile when others are crying?" There are always two sides of the coin and this idea is very important too. Empathy and compassion ARE VITAL for us to pull ourselves out of this "hole" we have created (a hole of suffering and pain) for only then (with empathy and compassion) will we STOP being violent to others for only then (you would think it would be easier than this and already happened but alas it has not . . .) ONLY THEN only then only then will we see the other person as our own hearts and through our own eyes and REALIZE that violence and hatred to another human being does absolutely nothing to further our evolution. So that leads us back to being happy. Yes, empathy and compassion to LEARN never to hate/judge/harm: yes, do that! At the same time increase your happiness and joy for as that soars so will you and as you soar so will humanity as a whole. Let us climb out of the dark hole we are creating as a species and realize the wholeness of oneness that we truly are.

And be happy too;

increase the joy and be happy.

TODAY'S MESSAGE

Do your best with what you have. Stay in the moment and take a good look at your feelings and your "energy" and the energies that come from the outer realms. Much of what we take on is not our own. Recognize it and let it go is always a good way to be. We cannot fix everything in this world. The best we can do is "fix" ourselves so we can be more loving and more caring individuals. When and as that happens we give out to the world a better and more compassionate energy; a better you/me/we. We are all one and most on this planet do not understand this idea. We get pushed and pulled and fight within our minds regarding what is right or wrong, who is good or bad and what in the world we are supposed to do while sojourning here on earth. Breathe Breathe Breathe Breathe. Recognize the changes in YOU. Work on YOU first to get yourself aligned and balanced. Breathe some more and bring in some gratitude: what a great time to be living here on earth amongst all these changes. It is not easy but it can be rewarding. You can't change everything around you but as you move more and more into your own shining light, you can increase the light in the wholeness of oneness called humanity. Stay strong. Find your core power and clear out the rest. Work on self and yet be a bit easier and kinder and gentler with self today. Breathe and smile. We are here; you are here: we are one.

Stay Strong!

LOVEANDLIGHT and have a blessed day.

TODAY'S MESSAGE

When you are feeling let down; when you are feeling things are not working out then go within. Go within to find the connection to source. Go within to find the light of life and joy: it is there within you. It is not on the outside; it can never be. It may seem like it sometimes when we say "if this would happen and if that would just come through then I'll be happy." This is just temporary anyway. Our time here is just temporary and any "solutions" are temporary. You are here and this is now and you will shine as you connect, connect, connect. Happiness or joy can feed you. Allow for it to come into your heart. As you suffer there creates an opening so if that is where you are then all hope is not loss for you can open that way. There are many ways to see the light. Look into a child's eyes: the light is there. Pray and be vulnerable and the light is there. Pet the dog and kiss the cat and more light will find its way into your heart. Life is up and down and again is just temporary. Your heart and your soul and your spirit is infinite. "Now" is infinite when you go within. All is here right here in the now. There is the joy and even in suffering we can find it. Be honest with yourself. Be honest and open and ask for more: more connection and more love and more understanding. This is why we are here. Have faith in this moment; have faith in yourself. Breathe and be and ask for more: more love, more love, more love.

You are divine.

Fear not!

TODAY'S MESSAGE

Life is perfect just the way it is.

There are the ups and downs but the ups can be so rewarding that sometimes you just need to wait for it, wait for it. Apply what you know. Apply the mystical practices in which you seek. Learn and apply is a good lesson for today. Release those others who are bogging you down. This "release" can be a simple cord cutting to let go of the energies that have bound you in the past. This is not "getting rid" of those people, per se, just allowing them and you to function with new energies and not the old energy patterns and programming (karma) of the past. When we live consciously there is less patterns and programming and karma to deal with. This is a goal in and of itself! Let's work with that today as well: cutting the old energy cords that bind (asking Arch Angel Michael or a deity/god/goddess/source of your choice) AND living and working and communicating and relating in a more conscious manner. Life is wonderful when you do. And you are wonderful to even be here during these turbulent times so thank you for that. So make the best of it! Clear up the old and fly high (yet grounded) in the new energies, the new earth ~ the new way to "be."

LOVE AND LIGHT and

have a blessed day.

TODAY'S MESSAGE

What are you learning? What are you learning about yourself today - about your interactions; about your place in this world and your purpose? We all serve different roles here on planet earth, and these roles may change at any given time. Sometimes we are the child and other times we are the mother of the child. Sometimes we are single and other times a couple and then single again. It doesn't matter!!!! What matters is what we are learning: the experience. It is all about being open for the lessons, for the joy of living and for the "exposure," if you will. There are so many things we can do here on planet earth and the most important thing about this idea is that you are here and you are doing it. Sometimes we take breaks and take a breather and just need to compose ourselves and/or incorporate what we've learned. Sometimes it is observation time where we gain understandings of what we want and what we don't want so that next time we can come at the situation a little differently (regardless of what that situation may be); moving away from the programming and away from our patterns that often do not serve us. The idea here is to just jump right on into that boat called life and give it a whirl . . . a really good try . . . a seriously opened experience and say, "yes, I'm ready to try it again. Here I am world; bring it on!"

Life is cool like that.

Go for it!

TODAY'S MESSAGE

When in doubt, trust yourself. Trust your intuition and guidance system. Better yet, ask to be given the required information and the "opening" for what you seek. There are many questions and many facets of "work" and how to be in this world. It gets confusing, right? So trust is a good thing to have and opening up to the unlimited abundance of the universe helps expand your world; your horizons. We all want to be in a world that is safe and yet at the same time many wish to expand their experiences to create, which sometimes may seem scary; unsettling. Sometimes we are in jobs that are confusing and relationships that are traumatic at worse, and dramatic at best. What to do; what to do? Trust. Trust your true heart and the intuition in your gut to guide you along step by step, sentence by sentence and each and every communication and action. Ask for the higher power/s (however you wish to view that) to give you even more ability to do so. Trust that life is worth living and love is worth doing. Trust that all is as it should be and when things seem "out of sorts" trust that it is still worth it. Life here on earth can be dark and cold and lonely. Life here on earth can be magical and mystical and full of gifts. Step into the later and be ready for the ride; the openings, the unfolding. For all is unfolding divinely. For regardless of the outcome, it is the ride, the experience and the joy in living that propels us to new heights.

Step up. It is time.

You are worth it. LOVEANDLIGHT!

TODAY'S MESSAGE

There are great things here on planet earth and great things in you. INDEED! Many times we feel so limited. Our dreams are limited and our desires and our creations. We've been beaten down and we just feel that things don't happen easily or are just impossible to do. An unrealistic dreamer, we feel, and/or have been called. Don't let this limit you. There is greatness in this world and greatness in you. It just needs to be unleashed! We are stifled, stifled, stifled, and stifled some more by fear. How much does fear limit you and your doings and growing and creations? This is all manmade and self-made fears. In truth the universe is limitless. Let us tap into the source of ALL, the source of UNLIMITED POSSIBILITIES, and make them OUR REALITY. Life is really as magical as that. Allow it; believe it; trust it and stay focused on self, love, light and the goodness of all things. We really are good beings . . . sometimes we just get mixed up. Sometimes others tell us our limitations and we believe them. If you feel limited, explore THAT and then move forward with faith and service: for the greater good; for the greater good of ALL. You are love and light and you are full of power.

Don't forget it.

Do something wonderful with your power today.

Love and light and God Bless!

TODAY'S MESSAGE

There is a time for every purpose under heaven. And though it may seem like "hell" sometimes here on planet earth we are truly blessed. Do you forget how blessed you really are? We are blessed, we are blessed, we are blessed for we have all we need and are learning and growing on this beautiful planet mother we call home (sometimes). Let us find gratitude in our blessings. May we find grace in our challenges and lessons. May we find an opening in our heart to give more and more love. Love is the power and the key to our survival. Love is the life-force power that sustains us. How much love do you allow in your day-to-day? Look around with the eyes of love and you will see love as the driving force of life itself. When people are in lack they lash out for they forget that it is LOVE that sustains us, not the "other things." We find many other things to occupy our minds and hearts. Much of this is material and attachments. We can all live a more beautiful life as we move away from the attachments that bind us to the physical "needs." Of course we have some needs but if we look around with loving eyes we understand we are blessed. The rest is just material head-games. The rest is away from love and it is love where we are headed so leave the past and attachments behind. Open up to the future with an open heart. You will find greatness there. It is not in the title, not in the job, not in the physical. Greatness is the life force that flows. Open up to love and enjoy some gratitude and the life force opens up to you. Have a Super Day and God Bless. You're doing fine! Don't-cha worry! All is well. All is well. ALL IS and it is all perfect; as are you.

TODAY'S MESSAGE

We are all one. This has been said before and deserves repeating. Many people vibrate on similar levels and others on other levels and we all make one humanity; one vibration. There is purpose for ALL of it. If we were all the same then what would we learn? There are many, however, that are suffering. They are stuck in their rut and they know nothing else. It is good for the higher vibrational people to give a little lift to those who are stuck. If that cannot happen, just being in the vibration of a higher realm/field can help those who are suffering. It doesn't take much: a smile, a glance, a gesture, a word. How much really will that make or break your day? You may find that it makes your day actually, as you spread the light, for the more you give the more you receive. Not only from the others, from the other humans who need a lift, but from above we gain more and more light. More and more love. The more you give the more you receive so don't forget to give. It is beautiful in and of itself AND it benefits the whole. We are all one so do help your brothers and sisters. They need it; they are waiting for you. One kind word; one gesture. ONE LOVE. Let us live this idea. Let us stop with the dividing. We are all worthy, all deserving. Kindness is the key. Compassion is in fashion. Let's lighten the load and help others. Stay strong in your light while at the same time sharing it. Let not the hate of the world take that away from you. You know the truth and the truth shall set you free: ONE HUMANITY; ONE LOVE; ONE LIGHT.

God Bless today and ALL days.

TODAY'S MESSAGE

Be not afraid. You are powerful when you tap into source. The source of all being-ness is endless in its knowledge and connective collective purposes. We are all pieces of the great being-ness and that one source is very powerful. The idea of using the power for the greater good is the way to be. Power for self-aggrandizement is not the way to be. You can be that way and this may work for you but in the end it isn't worth it, for ALL comes around in the end. The all is always working with karma and the circle of all things. There is the black and white and the dark and light and the heavy and the strong. There is good and evil and they are the flip side of the same coin. You can gain one and then need to see the other side. So "for the greater good" is a nice preamble for any prayer or manifestation for the increase in the source/knowledge/power is good for all and therefor better for the whole. This is not to say that you will get what you want when you want it. This is to say that there is EVERYTHING in the source and when you are tapped in you can better attain what you need. But what is it that you really need? We all need love and we all need to be cared for (fed and watered and sustained, if you will). It does not take much to have these things and many on planet earth (especially in the western societies) have a false sense of what is "required" to live. We have been selfish in many ways and that has put a burden on our livelihoods and our habitat (planet earth). Being conscious of what you want and need and allowing for the universe to provide helps balance that. Being loving brings you love and being charitable brings gifts from the universe. See how it goes around? It is as simple as that. Be loving and kind today just for the sake of the higher good and see what comes back to you in kind.

TODAY'S MESSAGE

Every day is a day for new beginnings. Lessons learned and moving forward. Sometimes we need to move back to move forward. Sometimes we need to look back with a new perspective to gain the clarity we need to release the old and be born anew. This is the idea that all (most) things can be seen as a nice lesson. Even the painful and even the harmful and even the most horrid human behaviors have lessons in them. We create ways of expressing in order to UNDERSTAND. Understanding isn't a quick and easy thing to do. True understanding of the way life works here on planet earth takes many lessons, many tries, and much "exposure." We cannot understand the beauty of peace without the opposite being seen and experienced. We cannot fully understand the gift of love without those times of indifference. We cannot comprehend the grace of faith without the need to be faithful; without those sometimes difficult and trying times. Many people don't like to be uncomfortable or to "work" but when we can look with new eyes we will see that much of the "negative" we've experienced has enhanced our growth in understanding the human experience. Then we are better for it and happier in the living experience. As we grow in understanding, notice the opening of the heart within you. The love there is great indeed (in – deed). Do be open to the awakening experience for as you do you unfold like the flowering lotus or the sparkling butterfly. Awakening the beauty of love, life and all that is. Blessings to you on this fine day.

God Bless.

TODAY'S MESSAGE

To live to the fullest we must be free. Free from the past and free from programming; free to love and freedom from fear. But how to get to that place one asks . . . how? Sometimes we are free-thinkers and free-lovers and brave hearts and at other times we "give up" and conform to the programming of the society at large. This happens and is fine for there is much in the way of denseness and structure here on planet earth. That is how it was designed and where we are at this point of our evolution. There is much freedom "taken from us" or limited TO us but there are some freedoms that can never be taken. We have free will and we CAN HAVE free thoughts and we SHOULD HAVE freedom to love. More love more love more love. For today let us look at our freedoms and lack-there-of. Let us not be angry in this regard but see how there are many archaic structures in place that limit us. These will change for we are becoming grander, broader, more open and accepting individuals. It will take time but it is on course. As we look at the freedoms let us look at the possibilities as well. An open and loving heart, a free mind, and free will where we can consciously make our lives a miracle: unlimited possibilities, one day at a time.

LOVEANDLIGHT and

stay strong!

TODAY'S MESSAGE

Every day is different. Every day has a different feel;
different energy. Things change out in the cosmos and
within our own solar system and that affects us
energetically/emotionally/spiritually/physically. This is all
fine and good for if there was no change there would be no
change and change is good: we need change. Therefore, for
today, let us enjoy the changing tides, the flowing winds:
stagnant is not the way to be for stagnation causes drowses,
death, disease. Action is where it is at; not reaction. One
can act by not reacting and doing nothing. If it is conscious
then this is a good thing. Being conscious is the key here as
we move and grow. The more conscious, the more we live
authentically. The more we live authentically the more we
"clean up our stuff" for we cannot live authentically when
we hide behind the masks and/or are cloaked in our sorrow,
pain and anger. Layers upon layers of old stuff: that is what
most of us live under. Let us break free from the past by
examining it and clearing it energetically, emotionally,
mentally, physically. Let us all be open to change and
growth and love and light. Let us ask the higher powers to
help us live in this way. Let the beauty of what you love, be
what you do. Find what you want to see in this world, BE it,
and then allow that new world of yours to manifest in front
of you.

It is there; bathed in light:

The New Earth.

TODAY'S MESSAGE

Love is where the heart is. This is a literal interpretation in the idea that as you focus on your heart space you will live more and more "in love" with everything. The time of the superpower brain energy is gone and the time for the supercharged love booster of the heart is where it's at. This is to say that you are love, you've come from love, and when you go back to love (living from the heart) you will shine more and more and your world we be all shiny too. Do breathe today. Take nice deep breaths. Do breathe in and out of your heart today and notice the body ease into alignment. Allow the fear in your belly to go; allow the chatter in your mind to go. Just breathe. In and out of your heart with gratitude of your life here on planet earth and all the beauty that living provides. There is greatness in you for as you go within you will feel and connect with the source of all things and that is great indeed (in deed). You are part of that source. USE IT! BE IT! There is such beauty here . . . find it . . . it is yours. The beauty of life is your birthright.

Yes, many are suffering and you can help them by being strong: strong of heart and strong in love and someone who is living to their fullest potential. The other stuff will work itself out. This is not saying to cast a "blind eye." This is saying to clear up yourself so there is more and more love to give. You have that power. LOVE AND LIGHT today and all days. One day at a time; one step at a time; one breath at a time (through the heart; through the loving heart).

And we proceed on.

TODAY'S MESSAGE

When we are in our heart space we are in a space of trust, faith; love. This sounds like a good place to be, doesn't it? When we live and breathe from this place/space, we can coast through the hurdles of life, for WHEN we are there, life will always feel sweet and flow freely. Life can be nurturing and wonderful. Life IS beneficial in many regards ~ we grow, we learn, we communicate. Sometimes we even play. Life can be full of love and playful situations/sensations. We need not take it "so seriously." We've all seen those master gurus that laugh and laugh at everything ~ we can have some of that lightness in our being as well! When we "practice" our methods of healing and love through meditation and yoga, through dance and art, through connections with others (human as well as those more earthly friends) we grow more and more open in the heart and more and more aware that all is PERFECT and life is a breeze. Breathe in this spirit; it is your birthright. Allow the sacred holy nature of the divine universe to enter your heart today: connect there, is the idea. Don't forget to practice your methods of enlightenment, for it is a practice. You will find an open space for laughter there; a space of joyous wonder. A love for living each breath: it is there within. Go. Find this place/space. It is waiting for you. And there you will remember who you are. There you will see and feel the connectedness of all things and you will be glad in it. LOVENLIGHT!

TODAY'S MESSAGE

Where is your focus? That is where your life IS for life is
perception and perception is where you are looking and
FROM where you are looking (what eyes/what
perception/what vantage point). This is the idea that if you
are "coming from a fear space" and looking at fearful things
then guess what your life is? Full of fear. See? Simple.
That is why hope is so important. Think of the perception
around hope? Coming from a happy place and focusing on
new beginnings . . . higher vibrational, compared to the first
example of fear, isn't it? The "problem" with hopeful
thinking is that when things don't pan out we often get
frustrated and angry; perception shifts and negativity ensues.
That is fine and dandy. Reevaluate what you want and
launch again. In addition to hope, add in some faith as well.
Faith is a different perception for there is a detachment of
results. Faith is kind of like gratitude in that regard: a
knowing that what IS, is special and important and perfect.
Faith and Hope and while you are at it, let's make it a trinity
by adding Love to the mix. With love we have that gratitude
feeling too in that we are thankful for what is in front of us
and we use the love as a means of communication and union
and not as a means to an end. That kind of love
(conditional) is not love. Love is love and straight up
beautiful . . . no need to get an outcome from it, just use it as
a powerful energy boost guiding all you do. Faith, Hope,
Love and no fear: let's do that today! God/Goddess/Source

Blessings for you today and ALL days.

TODAY'S MESSAGE

There is great love in this world. If you look around with loving eyes and be that love you wish to see it will show itself and there it shall be. It won't be on the news and in most you see on television and the internet but there is great love in this world nonetheless. The love is in your heart and in your connection to source. The love is in your heart and in your connection to those you love (family, friends, pets) and don't forget one's self-love is also a nice connection to get you into your heart/love space. There is great good in this world even though the world may seem to be falling apart around us. There is also much awakening even though we often see the "other side of the coin." This is fine and dandy and all is right in the world in this regard. For sometimes we need to realize what we don't want in order to focus on what we do. This can be seen in a simple form when it comes to jobs, relationships, self. It can be seen in a grander form when it comes to humanity. What do you want? How shall we live? Can you find it in self and then look and work through those eyes; that perception? That is the key here. That is something we can focus on today. If you want peace in the world find peace in your heart. If you want love then find that love connection. It is simple, really. Don't let the weight of the world take you away from living a peaceful loving life and extending that peace to all around you. Others may not have the capacity to stand strong in love and peace so you working on yourself to be able to do so is such a gift to the world.

You are a gift ~ don't forget it!

TODAY'S MESSAGE

Stay strong in your resolve. This is not to say to be stubborn or not be open to all the gloriousness of the universe; this is to say that we all need to stay strong in love and light. There is much happening here on planet earth and again, as has been said before, it can "make us" or "break us." The weight of the world can make us crazy, depressed, angry and/or withdrawn. It can put us in our beds where we don't want to come out and play anymore. We fear for the earth and her inhabitants and the safety of our livelihood. This is happening. Just recognizing this is the first and most important step. What is happening with you: thoughts, feelings, words? How does fear and uncertainty manifest in your body/mind/actions/reactions? Knowing this is the second step. We can take this information and allow our bodies and minds to lead us in whatever direction they feel more secure. OR we can stand up stronger than ever before in our beliefs of love and light and the goodness of living. What do these more lighter notes mean to you and how do they change your perception? That is another good question and another step to take. Taking it even further is the idea of living and loving to the fullest while being conscious, conscious, conscious and caring and supportive of self and others. Do take time to evaluate the way you react to fear and uncertainty. Do take time to process and then look at the beauty in your life and say thank you. A conscious thank you and conscious actions toward living a full and faithful life is where we can go from here.

Blessings to you on this fine day.

TODAY'S MESSAGE

Life is for the living. This has been said before but lets us
look at this again. Life is for the living, the
EXPERIENCING. The idea here is that all experiences are
good experiences and that has been said before so let's look
at that again. All experiences are good experiences despite
how they "feel" and how they appear for we are
experiencing and that is what it is all about. We grieve
deeply for the "state of the world" and this is happening
more and more to those aware and those unaware as well but
mostly to those aware. The "unaware" may be reacting and
feeling but those feelings are based on more reaction than
anything else and may often take the form of masks: anger,
sickness, confusion. The idea for those who are
experiencing grief due to the state of the world as we know it
is this: first identify that some of your feelings are coming
from outside of you. Notice how you REACT. Notice what
helps ease the pain (sometimes a mask and/or a medication
or even a "zoning out"). Notice how you love humanity so
much that you fear for their safety and the safety of Mother
Gaia. Now here is a trick you can try today: take it further
in . . . past the fear and past the grief/pain/sadness and go to
the love from which it stems. Love for the self and love for
life and love for friends and family and love for the earth and
love for whatever . . . then acknowledge this love, multiply
the love, and shine it outward. Imagine those you grieve
gaining the love and light they need from your pure heart.
Shower it out to the world. Imagine it and so it is.   LOVE
AND LIGHT TO YOU ON THIS FINE DAY AND
LOVE AND LIGHT TO ALL WHO ARE SUFFERING.

TODAY'S MESSAGE

We grow we change and sometimes we feel stagnant. It is fine. Sometimes we feel like we are back-peddling as well: that can be frustrating but that too is fine. There is great growth and change right now on the planet. This has been said before and I'm sure that each's perception changes around that subject depending on the day/time/space/place/frame of mind. The truth of the matter is that things are rocking and rolling here on planet earth and sometimes we feel caught up in the energy of the movement and at other times we feel like burying our heads for it seems too great of momentum in which to keep up. This is the idea of the single pounding wave on the shore versus the tsunami wiping out a city. See? Sometimes it feels too much but it is still energy moving and sometimes it feels "containable" while other times of course who or what can contain a tsunami. So what to do what to do what to do? Allow your own body rhythm to guide your actions. Allow yourself time to breathe and process when you need to. Pray and send love and light to all affected by the earth changes. Send love and light to Mother Gaia so she may continue to re-invent herself. Take heed, and stay strong, and then relax, and then reach for the stars and then take a nap . . . it varies for there is always so much to do here! Don't give up and bury your head though. Rest when you need to but stay present at the same time. Stay open for the changes and be glad in it. There is so much to be glad about in this big crazy world. Find something you appreciate; thank God/Goddess/Source/Earth Mother for it, multiply that feeling and shine it out to the world.

Love and Light Today and ALL DAYS.

TODAY'S MESSAGE

Take your time with things . . . process and understand.
Become more aware of EVERYTHING! This can take up
much time when we are aware of everything. Sometimes
that feels like an "overload" but in the long run there is a
new appreciation of life and our place here on planet earth.
This is not to say to "absorb" it all. The idea of the
"empath" is one that many people complain about and
suffer through. How can you have a greater awareness and
not take on the plight of the world? Concentrate on self and
your own feelings and understandings. Understand your
thoughts and feelings on war and starvation and these ideas
but taking on those roles for others serves you not and
doesn't help others much either. Don't let the weight of the
world drag you down to a place of sickness and non-action is
the idea here. Many of us are depressed with the state of the
world, the lack of "humanity" on this planet. This creates
feelings of helplessness and hopelessness. This world is
beyond hope and beyond help. That is a play on words for
your world is within you and the world's problems are
"without" you (meaning outside of you). Our main job is
self: cleaning up self and clearing and finding joy and
strength in spite of the outside effects. That is what can be
focused upon. Then you will have the strength and the
fortitude to help others; only then. See? In weakness and
depression we can only help so much; in strength and power
and love and light we can help more. Have a beautiful day
and God Bless.

KEEP THE FAITH!

TODAY'S MESSAGE

Did you know how important you are? Whatever you are doing ~ that is important. Whatever you are feeling: that is important too. Dreaming, conniving, conspiring, desiring: all important! Your body and mind and spirit: important. Your face, your smile, your words: important. You are special and you are worthy and you are lovely. It is important you are here on planet earth at this time. You chose to be here! Don't blame anyone but your own soul for this "contract" so maybe ease up a bit on that. Yes, things in this world are not perfect and things in general can "get ugly," but that is why you are here! All those important things about you make the whole of planet earth a different place BECAUSE you are here. Life if funny and awesome like that. Do take care of self during these changing times. Things are escalating and you feel it. Some feelings, most feelings, are simply indicators of other things and once recognized can be let go. Recognize! Awaken! Interact and take action! That does not mean that if you are having a quiet day not to stay quiet. Do what you need to do to take care of self! Why? Because you are so important here and life IS worth living. You chose to be here so remember why and take heed. The time is now. You are changing, the planet is changing and we are all getting stirred up. Stay strong in the light and at the same time care for self by listening to all aspects of yourself (body, mind, spirit). Love is the highest law. If nothing else cling to that.

Love and light and have a super day you amazing YOU!

TODAY'S MESSAGE

Life is for living; do not be afraid. Of course there are things we need to be cautious of in our day to day. We don't want to be reckless driving or standing out in a thunder storm. The idea here though is that being safe and thinking of self-safety is different than being afraid of things out of our control. Remember that beautiful prayer? God Grant me the serenity to accept the things I cannot change, courage to change the things I can and wisdom to know the difference? This is the idea. The media agenda is often one of fear. Fear mongering is not a pretty sight for it limits us in action, action, action. Working toward something greater despite the fear is always a nice lesson. As we work more and more in that energy then we may learn to give up the fear altogether. Doing nothing in the face of fear is limiting, of course, this is easily seen. Do you want to give up your light for someone else's agenda? No. Therefore, just take a look at what makes you fearful and with that fear what makes you powerless. Not only do we often stop our actions during fearful times (cower) but our minds go haywire and we ruminate all the things that may happen, over and over again. So another idea here would be that fear is False Evidence Appearing Real. Of course the evidence may not be false at all but it still may be limiting us as we stop acting and start reacting. See? Life is funny like that. So what is the cure for fear? Try some joy. Try some love. Try some acceptance and peace. Love and Light to you today and all days. Have a beautiful day!

NO FEAR! WHOOT!

TODAY'S MESSAGE

There are important things to do here on planet earth;

many of them you would not "think" would be so.

Life is interesting here and we have many interactions. How are you "acting?" It is good to be "action-ary" and not so reactionary. It is good to be as conscious as possible in all things. How are your interactions with family and friends? How are your interactions with significant others? What if everyone was a significant other: wouldn't that be an interesting way to live? Now, how are your interactions with animals and plants and insects? And how are you interacting with yourself: mind/body/spirit? Are you incorporating the trinity in all you do? Well, enough with questions: these are just ideas. Though as you think, so you create and as you create, so you be. Life is beautiful like that so dream away . . . don't think too hard (too critically) but dream that new way of living into your space and be glad in it. We are all significant and all interactions are important. You are significant and very special indeed so do remember to take good care of self. All is well in the world. You are perfect and we are working together to build a new world and your smallest interactions help us get there.

Are you ready?

Let's do this.

TODAY'S MESSAGE

Just be yourself. That is who you are and it is wonderful so just BE that. There are challenges at times and you can challenge yourself and be MORE than you thought you ever could be and that is a good thing too. But that you inside; that beautiful you . . . let that light shine out to the world. It matters not if you (feel you) are different than the masses or sometimes you feel you don't fit in. Maybe that uniqueness of you is what this earth needs right now. And as you are in your "you-ness" you'll feel better because you'll be living an "authentic" life. And it is great to be authentic and genuine as well. Why keep trying to fake it? We all need different things at different times and some of us (most of us) struggle. We struggle against ourselves and this makes us feel "less than." You are nothing less than yourself so if you are authentic and genuine then where is the struggle? This eases the tensions within. Forget the ideas you had as a child when you were looked down upon for you uniqueness. Embrace it now that you are stronger. You are perfect.

You are part and parcel of the great I AM and that uniqueness in you, YOU, may one day inspire the world. We all want to "be good" and "do good." We all "come in" wanting to give and to love. Just DO THAT in all the forms of you and step away from those who make you feel wrong. As you stand in your power, you will see less and less of those "naysayers" anyway. Do find the joy in living. This joy feeds your body, mind and spirit. Like a spark to the flame of your core essence, so too can be the joy lighting up your heart. May the beauty that you are, be what you do. Be YOU and enjoy (IN JOY).

LOVE AND LIGHT: today and all days.

TODAY'S MESSAGE

We are all one; we are part and parcel of the Great I AM. This has been said before but worth repeating. "Almighty I AM; Almighty I AM; Almighty I AM." Do know that repeating this "mantra" can be very powerful for it puts you in the "God Space" of infinite knowledge, health, perfection and light. It feels like love for when in this state you are pure love. The ego is not telling you to do this or that to make yourself better. It puts you in the now, in the being, and in the wholeness of oneness of God/Source/Love. We need more and more people to be tapping into source to "bring it down" here on planet earth where it is so dense. Here on planet earth we are "dense" and forget who we are. Let us make a vow to start remembering. We are love and light. We come from source. We are perfect right here and right now. Tap into the almighty power of love and light. Let the ego go as you show gratitude for the process. Be "full of self" in the way that you regain your power from source and allow protective mechanisms through prayer and ritual to keep you there; less affected by the outside scattery-sources: those who are confused right now and those who are depressed right now and those hanging out in their story. Stay "full of self/strength" through these processes so you may move forward in the light. As you stay strong and clear you will be more helpful to others. This is a simple idea: if you allow outside sources to "get you down" then of course you will have less strength and love for self and if and when you have less strength and love within then you have less to give. Stay strong in the light! Make that vow and start remembering: "Almighty I am; Almighty I Am; Almighty I AM." Love and light to you and yours now and forever.

BLESSINGS~

TODAY'S MESSAGE

Stay connected! Stay connected to the spark and soul of self
and the greater spark and soul of the divine source. There
lies your power. There lies your uniqueness and most special
life-spark and as you journey back toward source for
refreshers and refreshment and power, you can see the
beauty of all things: ALL THINGS! Love is the key to open
that door. Humble, broken, open and there you'll be,
pranamed at the source for more and more light. We are
light soul beings living in this dense thick (brained) body and
there is the yearning for more. Make the connection and go
there and gain more. It is your birthright to do so and your
growth and open-heartedness benefits you, the whole; the
source. We are all divine. Do not judge the other as you
proceed on your path. Say hello and stay strong and be
helpful but move forward regardless. If there is pain in your
heart and soul, look at it and work with it to release. Or
better yet, take it to the source and kneel humbly, broken,
open and just ask; just be. Simply ask to connect and be
open to receiving. All is well in this world and all is perfect
in you for you are indeed a spark of the divine light and love
of GodSourceOnenessWholenessLoveAndLight. Blessings
today and every day. One second at a time. Be easy on
yourself and just take it one second at a time.

All is well.

All is well.

TODAY'S MESSAGE

There is the idea of timing and patience. There is the idea of creating your own reality and your dreams. There is the idea of all things happening for a reason. How are you with all that? Sometimes it seems contradictory ~ these "new age" ideas. But of course all is perfect. The duality and the conflict in thought is all part of the process. What process, you might ask. Well, faith, for one. Faith and hope and love for three. Where do you want to be; what do you want to be doing? How happy are you living RIGHT NOW? How grateful are you RIGHT NOW for each breath, each step; each morsel of food in your mouth and each communication with another? THAT is where you can create your new world. By creating the gratitude, by doing the "gratitude work" can shift your perception to one of reward; to one of "life happening for you" instead of "to you" . . . and the internal resistance fades. When it creeps back in your noggin again, when it shows itself in your dreams or in your fears and feelings again, then STOP AND TAKE A LOOK. Oh, that again, you can say and then ask yourself: how connected am I right now? How can I become more connected (easy answer would be to meditate, breathe, ground, pray). Then ask yourself – in your deepest heart space: "do I have faith?" Ask to allow faith and hope and love to guide your every move. Most likely you DO HAVE FAITH – you just got side-tracked by something worldly. The mind can be easily distracted - that is why we should concentrate on working from the heart. Faith, faith, hope and love. Much of all to you on this fine day. KEEP THE FAITH and GOD BLESS!

TODAY'S MESSAGE

We are all one and on the path. We are individuals and yet
one; we are on "the path" and yet on our own. This is
perfect and in divine order. You don't want others to be
dictating your path, do you? Of course not. It is good to
keep this idea in mind. We are "programmed" to take a
certain kind of life-path from society and how we are raised
and from the media and how they can make money, make
money, make money. However, for many, this is not the
path we so wish to take . . . our path is our own and it feeds
our soul and we get depressed when we are not on it. "Let
me take my own path," our spirit screams! There is
something MORE THAN THIS! Yes, there is much more.
There is so much more than we can ever dream or imagine
and YET it is simple for it is ONE and we are ONE and so
it is. How can we stay strong and open and happy? Take
the steps you need to take on your path, consciously, and
with a wholeness of divinity. Divine wholeness; sacred
ONE . . . love eternal. All feeds the soul and feeds your
spirit and gives you strength in mind and body and we all
need strength in mind and body these days. Take your steps
consciously and with gratitude and be glad in it. If you are
frightened, access that and then make adjustments or let it go
OR take the steps anyway. Life can be funny like that.
There are choices we make consciously and choices we make
unconsciously (and/or reactionary). Whatever choice we
make consciously, whether it be "stay" or "go" or "left" or
"right" or crocked: it is all good for it is done it awareness.
It is all divine. It is all perfect; like you. Have a super day.
God Bless ~

TODAY'S MESSAGE

Your Life = Your Perception. Therefore, if you believe everything happens for a reason then it DOES! If you believe that the world is a cruel and evil place that is here to torment you, then it IS! So this is not trying to minimalize the dangers and cruelty of this world and living on planet earth and how difficult it can be. This is known and seen and "reported" ad nausea via the media. We are not saying it is not hard. We are saying that your attitude can change your life. Your perception/outlook/vibration/attitude/grace/forgiveness/acceptance and JOY can have an effect on how your life "rolls." So we can be stubborn and say "this world does not deserve my being joyful and I don't care if that will make me less happy; I just won't buy into this idea and shall stick to my own of this cruel, cruel world." Yes, we can do that ~ that way is perfectly acceptable and go for it if that is where you want to be. At the same time one can say, "I learned from that; that was difficult but it opened my heart; life here is full of beauty DESPITE the pain" and that would work too. When THAT "attitude" is in place, there is much less resistance, see? There is not the fighting within and the anger with the "out;" with your God or your idea of there being nothing above you; the anger and frustration with "your life" and your "circumstances," etc., etc. SOOOOO that can work too and it is entirely up to you. Are you open to receiving? That helps greatly. Are you open to change? THAT is a beautiful thing. Are you open for love and life? That is where you want to go for when you are open to the loving light of the "Great I AM Presence" then there is fullness and depth and breadth and glory in YOUR life. But is it up to you. It is entirely up to you . . .

TODAY'S MESSAGE

There is much time to do what one needs to do on their life's path. Never think that is too late to do. Take time to be "in your body" and enjoy all that love and life has to offer. Take time to communicate to the best of your abilities with others. Take time to nurture others and self and realize we have all the time in the world to BE whom we wish to be. Find and start BE-coming is a good first step and breathe into it. What is your ideal? What do you see as part of your life's purpose? Sometimes it seems too much to live in this way: the conscious way; the way of the path. But it isn't THAT bad and once we "get into it" then life flows more smoothly (this is not a guaranteed statement) but the idea here is to BE what your purpose IS and then things flow to you and life is provided in a way to create a stronger, bolder, more encompassing you. And again, there is enough time for all this. We do the best we can for where we are and then again, sometimes we must start again and try again and BE again. This is how it works for so many so don't feel you are the only one. There is a time to laugh, a time to cry, a time to live (do that now) and a time to reassess all we've done for learning and growing. Don't beat yourself up. Stay in your BE-ing and all works out in the end. We are sparks of the divine spirit. Don't forget that! Identify your spark and work on growing it stronger and brighter.

Like the fireworks we, together, light up the sky.

Have a blessed day and stay safe and strong in the light.

TODAY'S MESSAGE

Stay strong in the light. Proceed slowly and with intuition and yet not meekly but with grandeur. You are great: part and parcel of the great I AM Presence! Say it; say it again; say it again! Almighty I AM, Almighty I AM; Almighty I AM. Say it even though you may not mean it at first. The energy will catch on and you will begin to feel stronger. Stronger and stronger ~ that is where we are going. Lighter and lighter; that is evolutionary and our purpose(?). Is it our purpose to get lighter and full of love? Different people have different purposes here on planet earth but evolving is something that is happening whether we like it or not and whether we "strive" toward it or not. "Evolutionary" is the idea. So we just go on and be open and ask for strength and be open and ask for strength again and be open and accepting of life in general and your part in it, in particular. Ask to be guided and then listen. Ask to be of service and notice the opportunities. Be happy and notice the changes around you as you stand in your power and joy. Amma recently said we are to become warriors here on planet earth. Not the destructive kind, she added, but warriors of the light and love of source ~ carrying us forward in our evolutionary journey. Life is for the living and we live it and it is helpful to love it and we ask for strength and direction. Proceed slowly but with intention. Proceed as a warrior of light and see the changes. Almighty I AM; Almighty I AM; Almighty I AM. Yes, you are. You are strong and beautiful and everything is right with the world as you stand in your power of love and light. God Bless and have a safe day. NO FEAR! (Just joy).

TODAY'S MESSAGE

Stay strong in your light; in your spirit. Let the rest of the world be how they are and concentrate on self. You cannot help others feeling helpless and depressed. Keep your spirits elevated as high as possible and that allows a higher vibration in and around you. Find that which feeds your soul and go there. Find that spark in your core-being and activate that asking for increase power and strength to keep you whole and healthy. This can take many forms but the idea of keeping your trinity balanced (body/mind/spirit) is the idea here. Rejuvenate your body whenever possible and keep hydrated. Yoga is wonderful and finding yourself in nature or those of like-minds helps. This helps the mind of course to be with others of your ilk. Feed your soul in this way as well. Helping all people, animals, plants, things, and circumstances feeds your soul as well. Do those things that you know give you a boost of spirit energy: the outlet with the arts: song, dance, painting and literature. This place, planet earth, affords many beautiful things. Allow them to enhance your life. Don't forget they are there by being focused on all that you find wrong in the world. Don't forget those of like-minds; they can help you too. And as they help you feel stronger in spirit, you can help another.

Blessings, Blessings, Blessings and keep the faith!

TODAY'S MESSAGE

Keep breathing and stay grounded. All is right with the world. Do know that tragedy happens but do know that the media feeds us much more tragedy and fear compared to the awakening around the planet. Do you think it may be deliberate? To awaken and expand may be a threat to the old ways so let us leave the media on the back-burner on some days (it does not need to be taken away altogether) but do work on self and love and light as often as possible. The idea here is not to let fear control your life and your growth and to notice that much is manipulated in "keeping us down." We are souls in a physical body and we are becoming more light and love everyday regardless of the others who are staying stuck in the muck and mire. This is not to say that tragedies do not happen and that there isn't much needing to be changed here on planet earth: there is much needing to be changed here on planet earth. There is much heartache and pain and war and injustice. The idea is to not let it "take you out" or diminish you but to help you stay strong in your power of love and light so we can move THROUGH THIS and get to the other side where the majority will be ready to evolve and be closer to God/Source. Full of love and light and ready to create a new earth.

Blessings Love and Light to you on this fine day and stay strong ~

TODAY'S MESSAGE

Life is a journey. You are on a path. All is well with the world. Sometimes we stop and sit down on our path; sometimes we rest; sometimes we hide. Our path has twists and turns and oftentimes it has crossroads. Where to go; what to do next, we think. Take each step, one at a time, in great consciousness. Use your intuition to guide you to the next step. Use your heart and strength to keep you going.

Rest when you need to. Life is okay; we are here for a reason and it is truly "all good." As we progress on our path we learn these reasons for they present themselves over and over until we understand. On the other hand, we can decide how wish to proceed on our path and "who we wish to be" if we create an ideal for ourselves: how we wish to lead our lives. Do find your ideal and make it lovely, strong and meaningful. Do lead others into the ideals of love and light and compassion and grace. Find which words and measures resonate with you and make them your ideal and all will fall into place from there. Much guidance can be had in a simple ideal. When you are at a crossroads then remember the ideal and go in the direction that works toward that. See? We are all infinite and loving and wonderful. Many forget. Let us make it our life's purpose to remind those who have forgotten that we are all one. We are all one.

We are one.

LOVE AND LIGHT and have a blessed day.

TODAY'S MESSAGE

Life is full of ups and downs. Much happens in the astral forces and universal forces that we do not see, nor understand. Though often times we feel these things and they do affect us physically, mentally and emotionally. That being said, what do we do? Well, the best thing to do is stay within the body system and learn from there. Let not others tell you what is what and who is who and who to hate and what to do . . . do know the information is inside of you. At the same time, when you have information that may help others, do share it when necessary. The idea though is to stay strong within self; to ground into mother earth; to ask for the best course of action in any given circumstance and to believe. Believe in the great spirit of Mother Gaia. Believe in the true nature of you, a divine being here on planet earth. Believe that there are higher forces at work and that you are strong. Believe and have faith in the Source/God/Goddess/Goodness of Oneness. Believe that we are moving toward beautiful enlightenment. Believe that you are special just the way you are. Enjoy this earth/spirit/life and find joy in ALL you do. We are each here for a reason. Find that reason and expand your heart/strength/chi; shining it out to the world with all your gifts. Life is for the living. Be not afraid to live it to the fullest. Be not afraid to be your authentic self. Be not afraid from the media circus.

BE you. BE strong. BE-lieve.

TODAY'S MESSAGE

Do work on self and yet have a good time while here on
planet earth. There is much to see and do here and to
ENJOY (IN-JOY). How much joy can you infuse into your
day? How much play and laughter and light? These things,
this energy, feeds our souls so do allow THAT for yourself
and your life. We are all here for a brief time and then we
shall venture elsewhere. This is a special planet with
wonderful opportunities for learning and growing. There are
a variety of energies of people here working on various
paths. We meet them and we learn and grow just by being in
their presence regardless of "where they are" on their
journey. Do keep YOUR energy up and high-vibrational by
joyous living and strong work on self through meditation
and yoga and all the amazing simple tools we have at our
disposal. Walking in nature . . . thanking the sun, the moon
and the earth. Thanking Mother Earth and Father Sun and
thanking YOUR mother and father and all who have helped
create this experience for you. Some of us relent over our
"difficult childhoods" and all our traumas . . . this is not to
diminish "these issues" ~ the idea here is to celebrate YOUR
LIFE now as often and as consistently as possible. Let the
old go with forgiveness and a new knowing/awareness. This
idea can even be thought as a selfish act: whatever has
happened to you and however much pain you've
experienced in your life ~ the sooner you can fully let that
go, the clearer and happier you can be. So just do it and live
free. Have a blessed day. God Bless.

TODAY'S MESSAGE

There are always the wax and the wane; the push the pull; the yin and the yang. Do try to know this when "going through" some down-time. There are oftentimes when we need to "regroup." Nature does this too, so it is good to be aware that this is a natural thing. This receding is something we just need to accept to the best of our ability in order to move (jet) forward once again when we are ready. Sometimes life throws something in our way where big changes must occur in order to move forward again. This can come in the form of illness, disease, an accident, a divorce, etc. etc. There are countless ways this can happen. These times are obvious of changes required and we move through them to the best of our ability with the options that come up. Other times there is a nagging in our souls/hearts that feel like we must make changes in order to move forward. These occurrences are more subtle so the resolution regarding the changes seem subtle (murky sometimes even) as well. These are times where giving yourself "some time to process" can help. Do take time to process your thoughts, feelings, fears and relationships. Don't beat yourself up over (or during) the process. It is a process! Everyone goes through these times. It is life and it is natural. Ebb and flow. Propelling forward and then receding back. Like the breath: in and out - we need both to live. We are in a time of great change. Do allow changes that appear in your life to flow as smoothly as possible. Give yourself time and ask for smooth transitions and obvious signs and answers! We have all the time in the world and the universe wants to help. Be strong and courageous and have a blessed day. PEACE OUT!

TODAY'S MESSAGE

Look around you and take it in. There is life all around us
and it is vibrant. If you happen to be out in nature look
around again and feel the vitality: the life-source reflective in
all things green and growing. At the beach you feel the
waves pushing and pulling and being happy in their dance.
If you happen to NOT be out in nature, you can "tap in" by
simply using the mind during meditation "finding your safe
place in nature" to imagine and ground there. Much of our
perplexed mind is due to the distance from the natural. In
nature there is balance and it becomes reflective in our
body/minds/spirit. Away from the natural element we go
off kilter: sometimes a little and sometimes a lot. What to
do? What to do? If you can't get out into the elements you
can intend them into your heart/self. Feel the fire, the
water, the air and the earth. Connect them to your body
elements: air in the lungs, water in the
blood/organs/muscles, earth in the bones, and fire in the
core/belly and the head. Use the earth elements in
connection with your body to rebalance. Take off your
shoes and feel the ground beneath you. Connect there. Put
your hands to the heavens and connect there. Earth, water,
air and fire are part of nature and part of you. We are one
with her. That thought/idea/commitment helps in the
reconnecting. There are many ways to connect to the earth
mother; this is just one. May you find your toes in the
earth/sand/water/grass (soon, if not now). May you look to
the heavens and say a blessing in honor of the sun. May you
be grounded and healthy on this beautiful day embodying
the earth elements. And may you have a blessed day, today
and every day. God Bless.

TODAY'S MESSAGE

There is a time and a purpose for everything:
EVERYTHING!!! Do know that all is well in this world
and even though things may not seem "all well" in your
world, it probably is. We worry about others and we feel
their pain. This hurts and we get saddened at the difficulties
being faced by our loved-ones and our friends. But we do
not know the purpose for these struggles nor the lessons
learned nor the gifts. There are many gifts that are given
even in sickness and struggle. Oftentimes during these
difficult times we turn inward and learn new lessons and gain
faith and love and so much understanding. We cannot walk
in another's shoes nor be in "their skin" so we do not know
their processes. All we can do is work on our self, our faith,
our lessons and learn to love even more; even more; even
more . . . and a bit more even. When times are tough take a
deep breath and know that we are one. Send love and light
to all who need it! Ask for protection from the highest of
high to secure our hearts in the brightest of light. Ask for
guidance and then look for and be open to receiving it. That
is all we need to do. There is a time and purpose for all and
you are doing a fine job. Keep up the good work and
remember joy.

Be open for it . . .

**there is love and faith and joy in all things and as you
open, more will come.**

Keep the faith!

TODAY'S MESSAGE

Love is the answer; love is the key.

One needs to find the love and then create the space for forgiveness, for understanding and for compassion for those around us: animal, plant, mineral, sky and gifts of this earth (along with all the people). We are all part and parcel of the Great I AM ~ that of the earth planet and that of the higher realms/universe/source. WE ARE PART OF SOURCE! We are part of SOURCE and here on planet earth representing the same. How are you representing your GodSelf/Goodness while here? It is not easy to be Godlike and Godloving/Compassionate while here, for things can feel very dense and we feel "less than" and become fearful, due to things we don't understand. That is the first work ~ finding yourself as God/Good and to be not afraid. Let us work on being not afraid as we grace ourselves here on earth. Let us be Godlike and be not afraid to shine that brilliance of ONENESS upon the nation, upon the people; upon the world. Be kind to self for you ARE part and parcel of the Great I AM and you are IMPORTANT! How important you are ~ can you grasp this? Can you grasp the idea that you are here to shine your light? Are you able to grasp that your happiness allows more light to shine within and without? This is you: a brilliant light! This is you: a divine ambassador here on earth! This is YOU: LOVE! Please let it shine; please let it shine; please let your SOUL LIGHT SHINE. You are the light of the world!

Shine!

TODAY'S MESSAGE

Release the fear that holds you back. We all hold onto fears
from our past life experiences. They can be viewed as
guideposts on "what not to do" but more often than not,
they simply add up and create a larger sense of "I'm not
good enough." These things can go. We can ask for a
release of "all that does not serve us." This is our right and
with strong intention, so it shall be. We can walk in the
guidance and abundance of the universe. We can reach our
highest potential. We can live a life of freedom of fear and
"misguided" thoughts. We can do these things; YOU can do
these things, but it takes a conscientious effort. It takes
forethought and fortitude and COURAGE. We often define
ourselves by our accomplishments and our failures. Where,
instead, we COULD let go of these labels and connect more
fully, flowing with the divine light of oneness. It takes a few
steps up, however, to get to this flow and the releasing of the
past is a good way to start. Breathe deep and connect.
Release fully and you will find you are floating a bit higher
than before. THERE is the flow of the divine presence,
now more accessible to you. It is simple to see from this
perspective. When we are weighted down and afraid, our
possibilities seem limited. When we are free of our fear, the
sky is the limit. See?

This is something we can work on today.

LOVENLIGHT!

TODAY'S MESSAGE

Finding peace within is pivotal during these changing times. Life can seem challenging these days and often times confusing. When anger boils within your heart ~ find the triggers and work them out. There is enough anger and hatred in the world today: we don't need it festering there in your heart. We need the heart-space for navigating during these challenging times. We need to start living from the heart and less from the mind in order to evolve here on planet earth. Any anger or resentment or confusion or whatnot is just holding you (and all men) back from moving forward. There is light here. Find it. There is love here: use it. There is hope here: BE it. The glory of life and living and god/goddess/good presence is all around you and if you don't see it then that is fine. Go to the heart-cave. Look for it and clear out the rest. You will see a light shining in and throughout and that is where you shall find your peace. Of course we as humans delve in and out of the peace state because there are great changes here and we need to "see" better so oftentimes anger and resentment and other things may come into our existence so we can be aware of them. THEN we can start clearing them out. THEN we can start letting them go. All we need is an openness and willingness to learn and grow and live in the divine presence. The rest is a process. Sometimes it happens quickly but most of the time it happens in steps and stops and starts. Be easy with self and find the love in your heart. It shall sustain you. God Bless today and every day.

LOVENLIGHT!

TODAY'S MESSAGE

Take stock in all your gifts. Do use them wisely and generously. Find those things you do that light you up to fuel your fire, your soul, your laughter. Allow more light to grow as you learn and grow by using that which gives you joy. Do know that joy is powerful. Do know that you being joyful gives you strength and even more joy. Do find joy in all you do. Know that some things come as challenges in this life but in a past life may have come easily. Some strengths come from past lives if we ask for them. Of course, some lessons come forward from past lives as well. Do know you have access to infinite possibilities by tapping into the soul source. This is your birthright and can be done at any time; not just in times of struggle. Do know that the universe is abundant and you will be cared for. Ask and you will receive. Do not fear for we have enough to go around. You are enough as you are and this world IS moving forward despite outward appearances. Breathe and enjoy your gifts. That is all you need to do. And remember to ask when you are in need. Connect and breathe and ask. Rest assured; all is perfect ~ as are you in all your brilliance and glory.

God bless and be safe.

Be happy.

There is no reason not to.

TODAY'S MESSAGE

You have everything you need. Right within is your happiness. Around you is everything required to live here happily on earth: the universe provides this for you. Tap into the unlimited abundance of the universe for everything else. Release judgment of how things are "supposed to be" and become one with IT ALL. Of course this takes practice and sometimes we resort back and try to hold onto that which we feel is right and just. We know not the ways of the world and the higher realms so we cannot adequately decide what is right and just for the world and even ourselves: we don't have a universal picture, if you will, of what that would be. Trusting helps get us more to the universal picture though our human minds still, most likely, will not understand. So we trust and we move on. So we trust and we do the best that we can. We trust and we allow karma and universal forces of yin/yang, give and take, and higher thought to provide. Love is the way to get to the trust idea. Love and faith; caring for others and hoping/dreaming/manifesting a better tomorrow. Stay focused on putting self back together first. Keep fixing self and the universe will "fix" the rest. Everything is perfect.

We are on a journey.

Enjoy the ride.

God/Goddess and Goodness Blessings to you today and all days.

LOVENLIGHT!

TODAY'S MESSAGE

Concentrate on self and your interactions with the world.
Live YOUR IDEAL (soul purpose/main focus) and let
others live theirs. Worry not for the ways of men and who
said what and to whom. Worry (or better yet focus upon)
YOUR ACTIONS and reactions. Make less of what others
do and more of your conscious responses. The idea here is
to "RE-act" less and ACT more (in consciousness ideal
loving life thought process) of who you are and what you
want to present to the world. We can do many more
favorable actions when we act and not react. We can create
great beauty when we worry less of others actions and focus
more on self-in-the–world. See? This is not to say to not
enjoy other's kindness and be grateful of such. This is not to
say to not try, in your greatest ideal loving power, to get
along with others in this world and find understanding. This
is to say that YOU living peace and love and whatever
YOUR ideal is, can be the focus of any given day. This is
not to say to try to bend people to your will, either. This is
conscious living of love. This is gratitude for where it takes
you and for others involved. This is YOU standing in
YOUR POWER of love and joy and letting no man put
these asunder. This is not selfish; one can BE more and DO
more lightwork when focusing on living in this way: less
reactive; more conscious being. Only then can we change
the world. Only then.

One heart at a time.

YOURS.

TODAY'S MESSAGE

All days are lovely ~ it all depends on how lovely you make it. The idea of feeling good and feeling happy lays (mostly) with the individual. Each of us, when "trained," has the ability to turn their feelings around, to make themselves "better," and to live in the loving embrace of life and the world. This sounds simple but it is not ~ it takes great practice. The idea here is that YOU DO have much ability in how you "feel" during each and every day. Many people pick up "other energies," outside of themselves, and those energy effects the mind and body. So again, looking at that, deciding if those feelings and thoughts are coming from you, and if so why, and if not how/why and then make a conscientious choice to resolve, change and elevate that which you perceive as your life and your interactions within it. ALL is PERFECT! I am healthy. I am happy. I can do anything. See how these thoughts seem to elevate, in comparison to say, "I am sick, I'm so unhappy, I can't do anything." Yes, there is a great difference. So DO use your tools. DO find strength from within and change your "without" by using positive affirmations. DO meditate, do yoga, stay vigilant in your practice. DO find something to be grateful for today; there is always room for that. DO rest if you need to. DO be kind and loving. DO never EVER give up hope. DO stop any negative self-talk. DO laugh and be joyous. LOVE AND LIGHT and have a lovely day!

God Bless.

TODAY'S MESSAGE

Come down. Come down from the clouds into your heart. Come down from your head into your heart. Leave the commotion and find your focus on your heart space of love and light. This sounds simple to do and/or it sounds fantastical, but in reality it is a practice. We can practice living from the heart space by placing our focus there.

Oftentimes our heads are out in the ethers or we are constantly in thought mode. Sometimes we are "out of our bodies" completely. This is easier to happen these days with the change of energy/vibration/situations. So again, just a concept here, and one that needs to be practiced but a good practice for today: BREATHE. Again, sounding silly sometimes and too simplistic to work. BREATHE (anyway). Let the thoughts go. BREATHE DEEP. And again comes the thoughts of doubt, ego; blame. Release and BREATHE. Connect to your heart. Let the rest go. Find YOUR space of connection and stay there for a minute as you BREATHE. This is not a reward for "living in this chaos." This is a daily practice that can be sustained throughout the day. When we "go there" and we "breathe there" and we connect there, we feel good, we feel right, we feel like our soul-selves, full of heart; full of love. Let us find ourselves there as often as possible today. Let us connect. Let us be liberated from the chaos around us by finding our heart and living from that sacred space of LOVE. And LIGHT. It is our birthright. We CAN live from this space. Go there and **BREATHE.**

Enjoy! In – Joy.

AMEN.

TODAY'S MESSAGE

All things happen in their own timing. Unfortunately we, as humans on this planet, often don't know what time that is. That is funny and exciting when the universe works like that. Sometimes it works to "our favor" and sometimes it seems not. Maybe it is always working to our favor. Maybe we just can't see the big picture? We can't see the forest for the trees. Maybe when you are stuck in traffic, the universe just saved you from an accident? Maybe when you forgot to take the trash out and return to do so you were put in the perfect timing of something else entirely! We don't know. We never will know. We don't have to believe that this is true for it to be true. However, if we believe the universe is working with us, FOR us, then we can relax a bit: take a "chill pill," if you will. Many are in the hurry, hurry mode. While others are slow during the winter/hibernating months. Many are confused about what to do next. Are you feeling confused? Having faith in the universe and trusting, at the same time having VISION, is a good place to be when it comes to manifesting your gorgeous destiny. Sometimes we look back and are surprised at the miracles the universe put into play for us. Some may call it "happen chance" while others feel gratitude regardless and are simply happy being here. Being thankful and being gracious and being love and loving makes life so much more enjoyable. Do try to work from that realm today; do try to be in that space of love and willingness and graciousness and beauty. All in due time, as they say. Find perfection in the NOW and more perfection will gravitate to you. BLESSINGS LOVE AND LIGHT AND HAVE A WONDERFUL DAY!

TODAY'S MESSAGE

How are you feeling and thinking and being? This of course fluctuates each and every second of the day. Do know that thoughts and feelings can be fleeting and/or will not remain always. Not only that, much (all) of your thought patterns are under your control. That being said, one can change their feelings (for the most part) by changing their thought patterns. This again is under your control. Now being – that is another story altogether. Being. Being. Being. Knowing and glowing and dancing in the light: being. Sometimes in the being we feel strongly and think deeply and other times we let go and enjoy joy to the maximum capacity. The idea here is to clear what you can when it comes to thought patterns. Notice your random thoughts and link them with the feelings (which can vary considerably and quickly). Find the root thoughts and change those around. As you let the thoughts go, the more being will come and the more spontaneous joy. We can think ourselves into joy too for thoughts are things. Watch your thoughts –this is important right now. Sometimes deceptive-joy-thoughts aren't the best thing for us either. Truth; light; gratitude and a sincere willingness and openness to healing and change and love, are the greatest things you can do for yourself and your world today. Do not give up hope: this is a process and we are all "in it." Some as you see are struggling while others are escalating. Let neither effect you for you are you and your process is yours alone. Just as your thoughts are yours and your responsibility. Do enjoy your day and watch your thoughts; find the triggers and the programming. Be in love. That is a good place to be today and every day. Love and light ~

17347951R00092

Made in the USA
Middletown, DE
19 January 2015